Insider Secrets to Internet Safety

Advice from a Professional Hacker

SMILING EYES PRESS

by

Terry Cutler

SMILING EYES PRESS

3440 Provost
Lachine, Qc
Canada H8T 3J6

Manufactured and produced in Canada

ISBN Paperback: 978-1-7771119-0-8

Proofreader: Dounia Royer
Editors: Dounia Royer & Richard Tardif
Cover Design by: Laurie Roche
Interior Book Design: Richard Tardif
Printed in Pointe-Claire, Quebec, by Business Box

Dedication

To my wife Franca, thank you for all your support while putting up with me and taking care of the kids while I was building my company. It wasn't easy, I'm sure. I probably made it tempting to strangle me and hide the body, but you rarely let it show. Instead, you were always patient. Your words of encouragement and love sustained me. You are the main reason for this book.

Thank you to our sons David and Matthew, my parents Diane and George and my sister Karen-Ann for their support, hugs, kisses, and unconditional love over the years, which helped me persevere.

Acknowledgments

Meeting *Laura Chappell* of Chappell University back in 2004 at the Novell Brainshare conference in Salt Lake City is where my passion for Internet Safety for Kids was born. In her presentation, she spoke about how she posed as a teenager lured by Internet predators and how she was able to assist law enforcement track them back, which was all I needed to alter my career path. If it wasn't for Laura, this book, the online courses, or in-school presentations to parents and kids might not have existed. Thank you, Laura, for your continuous help and guidance in our industry. You are a true leader.

Thank you, *Pete Herzog,* for being part of this book and my legacy. I wanted you to be part of it because I consider you a pioneer in the cybersecurity industry with your work on OSSTMM and Hacker Highschool. Our values are aligned, especially with keeping kids safe and educated online. Keep up the great work.

Thank you to *Loui Kasimatis.* Your advice and guidance on keeping things simple have helped me get clear my mind of clutter.

Special thanks to *Richard Tardif,* my good friend, mentor, ghostwriter, motivator and CEO of Smiling Eyes Press, to get this book done. Thank you for your willingness to help me, especially in polishing my writing skills.

Thank you to *Dounia Royer* of Smiling Eyes Press for her attention to detail and comments when reviewing this book. The book now reads much better than I expected, so much so I'd be willing to pay for a copy of my book. Well done!

TABLE OF CONTENTS

FOREWORD

Winners don't quit, and quitters don't win. But if you neither win nor quit, you likely work in cybersecurity. To most people, cybersecurity seems straight forward, but that's because of tireless crusaders like Terry Cutler diligently working to break it down to its essence. It's tough. I know, because I'm a long-time cybersecurity researcher.

Terry reached out through an email in 2008 regarding the Open Source Security Testing Methodology Manual (OSSTMM), a project in which I was involved. I noticed the Novell domain. If you don't know or remember, Novell was the first known network. Novell was the thing before Microsoft and Apple networks became a thing. That was the thing that got you on this new Internet back in the early nineties.

I replied to Terry's email. He was polite, but I expected that with him being Canadian. We continued to exchange emails over the next few years. Novell faded, and Terry moved on to companies where he grew in knowledge and reputation. Had I not seen that email from Novell, we would likely not have gotten to know each other or collaborate on projects.

Cybersecurity is challenging.

There are more ways for a cybercriminal to creep through a 20-person network than there are hydrogen atoms in the known universe. Chess games have fewer moves.

There are thousands of indeterminate types of interactions between people and systems across data networks. Telecommunications, wireless communications, applications and human contact, can occur in infinite combinations both inside and outside a network. It can be random or malicious. It can be annoying and devastating. With that many combinations, it isn't easy to defend.

Which makes cybersecurity a grind because it requires constant attention to details making sure security grows as infrastructure grows. If security doesn't grow, the opportunity for a threat is exposed. Which is why we say cybersecurity is the place where you can't quit, but you can't win as there are always new threats.

That's why Terry wrote, Insider Secrets to Internet Safety: Advice From a Professional Hacker, his first book.

Terry is invested in cybersecurity and how to explain it in a way people can understand. One thing is knowing cybersecurity, and the other is being able to help others. We're all in this together.

In cybercrime, attacked at home or in the corporate world, every victim becomes a cash incentive for the hacker, not only in the present but in the future. Every loss makes the bad guys more powerful. Professional hackers like Terry can protect, research and teach us how to defend ourselves.

Terry Cutler's book, Insider Secrets to Internet Safety: Advice From a Professional Hacker is a book you should read.

Peter Herzog
Security Researcher and Ethical Hacker

Testimonials

"Terry is one of those gems in the IT world – someone who truly cares about his customers/students. We have known each other for many years and have many mutual interests in the security industry. I am completely confident when recommending Terry to my customers and colleagues – I know he will get the job done right!" - *Laura Chappell, Owner Chappell University.*

"Terry is a very talented support professional with a particular skill bent in "white hat hacking" He's well respected in the security community and really does know his stuff. His work has been published in national newspapers and he has appeared on radio explaining information security for the layperson. Terry is keenly interested in growing his skills in security particularly and brings great enthusiasm and aptitude to this important area." - *Ross Chevalier, CTO Novell.*

"Terry is a very knowledgeable individual with great networking and technical expertise. I have had the pleasure of collaborating with him on several information security related matters and look forward to much more in the years to come." - *Ralph Echemendia, - CEO Seguru.*

"Terry has been a long-time advocate and friend of Core Security. He has taken every opportunity to promote Core at industry events, at customer sites and even on TV. His deep understanding of the product enables him to clearly articulate the business value of the product, while ensuring that its technical capabilities are full addressed." - *Mike Yaffe, Director Marketing Core Security.*

"Terry Cutler is a passionate individual who has been known to invest an incredible amount of effort to ensure his customers receive the best possible attention when a software crisis affects their networking infra-structure. Terry is not averse to sacrificing his own personal time when it means the difference between success or failure of a customer's operations. Since roughly 2005 Terry has been fascinated with IT security, and has invested significant personal time to earn his credentials as an Ethical Hacker. He has since been cited in several articles for this expertise, including local newspapers. I have watched Terry grow through his career at Novell and am proud to see where this adventure has led him." - *Richard Cabana, National Security Advisor, Novell Canada.*

"Terry Cutler is one of the most valuable people I have ever worked with. Experienced Ethical Hacker that's Terry Cutler! That's him – open minded, multi-skilled, dedicated and precise strategist. Experienced and honest co-worker, a person you can trust when you want to be sure that important tasks will be completed in a systematic and precise way. I enjoyed working with him on the various projects we took on." - Woody Ghsoubi, Senior Technical Lead, Digital Locksmiths, Inc.

"Terry was a guest speaker at the Ottawa Chapter International Association of Administrative Professionals (IAAP) presenting on "How Hacker's Pick YOU". His presentation was extremely informative and eye opening for many of us working in the administrative field. It also provided us with great information we could take home for use within our family life. We hope to hear him speak again at a possible future IAAP event!" - *Helene Larocque, Administrative Assistant, Children's Hospital of Eastern Ontario*

"In my role at the Lester B. Pearson School Board, I work to link business and educational partners to teachers and students of the Lester B. Pearson School Board. A very important and essential program brought forward at the LBPSB by our Educational Services team was "Digital Citizenship", allowing teachers and students to better understand the importance of bringing forward the ethics of digital citizenship and the importance of understanding that our digital footprint is with us for life. As a part of our program, we created a focus group which included business partners, teachers, administrators and other educational partners to better understand "what it is we wanted our students to know about ethical digital citizenship" when they entered the workforce. Terry Cutler was a member of this focus group and provided such valuable information to all of our committee members about internet security and safety. Terry has spoken since then to many groups of students and teachers about internet safety, and has given valuable information for us to write guidelines for the importance of internet safety for our youth today. Terry is a true professional who is always willing to help by sharing his tremendous expertise in this field with our teachers and students. He is extremely knowledgeable and willing to take the time to listen to the needs of the schools." - *Nancy Battet, Partner Liaison, Lester B. Pearson School Board.*

"When it comes to digital security, Terry Cutler is the most knowledgeable person I have ever met. Always helpful and insightful, Terry saved us a tremendous amount of time and money with our server security issues. If you suspect that you have been hacked, or better still, if you want to prevent being hacked, I highly recommend that you contact Terry." - *Hagai Maidenberg, Innovative Leadership, Strategic Planning, Product Vision.*

"As a computer security student, I often read the blog written by Terry Cutler and find it helpful in expanding my knowledge in the IT Security field. He is truly an expert in his field and his articles are informative, most simple to understand and the best part of it is that I can relate it to my studies." - *Tharmini Janarthanan, Cyber Security Researcher* wormed. "NASDAQ" originally stood for "National Association of Securities Dealers Automated Quotations" and it's considered the largest electronic screen-based equity securities trading market in the US and second-largest by market capitalization in the world. As of January 13, 2011, there were 2,872 listings, and the trading company has more trading volume than any other electronic stock exchange in the world.

And on February 5 of 2011, NASDAQ OMX officials reported that they had discovered what the Fortune 500 Company called "suspicious files" and "dubious intrusions" on their servers, but that these were unrelated to NASDAQ's trading systems.

During the company's routine security monitoring, it spotted those suspicious files loaded onto the US Web-servers, which had no connection with its trading systems. It discovered that it's web-portal running the Directors Desk software had been harmed. The Stock Exchange instantly investigated with the help of external forensic companies along with the top US law enforcement. Experts immediately deleted the files. Hackers had neither accessed nor obtained any customer information from the Directors Desk.

"So far, [the perpetrators] appear to have just been looking around," reported the Wall Street Journal in March of 2011. The WSJ broke the story saying NASDAQ's computer network had been broken into, specifically a service that allows leaders of companies, including board members, to share confidential documents securely.

The NASDAQ situation set off alarms within the US government because of the exchange's critical role, which officials put right up with electric power companies and air traffic controllers. Other infrastructure components compromised in the past included a case in which hackers planted potentially disruptive software programs in the US electrical grid.

"It was inevitable," said Justin Magruder, then chief executive of Noetic Partners, which builds trading data systems. Magruder made the comments in FinancialTimes.com, meaning there is a vulnerability because of the sheer number of access points. "Many have already been hacked. We don't hear about it."

We did hear about the "flash crash" in US markets that same year, triggered by an algorithm in the futures markets which malfunctioned, sending the Dow Jones average down 1,000 points – and back up again – in 20 minutes.

NASDAQ officials said that the "web-facing" application, called Directors Desk, was potentially affected by hackers of unknown origin. Tech-savvy hackers breaching American exchanges may threaten the savings, pensions, and retirements of middle-class families across the world, and it shakes the foundation of the unstable and recession tottering markets.

Directors Desk, an online registry founded in 2003, is considered a web-based "cloud" application capable of storing data for up to 10,000 companies, many in the Fortune 500 realm, according to its website. The registry provides multiple levels of protection to guard clients' confidential data against undesired access. Such a standard includes employee background screening; policies that restrict physical and logical access to classified information; management of information systems; firewalling; intrusion detection, risk assessment; and guaranteed destruction of expired data.

It may not have been enough because the hacking of financial institutions was on the rise. Computer hacking is a problem for many countries.

The US authorities have dealt with cyberattacks linked to computers in Russia, China and Eastern Europe.

Tom Kellerman, a former computer security official at the World Bank who later worked at a firm called Core Security Technologies, said the most advanced hackers in the world are increasingly targeting financial institutions, particularly those involved in trading.

"Many sophisticated hackers don't immediately try to monetize the situation; they frequently do what's called local information gathering, almost like collecting intelligence, to ascertain what would be the best way in the long term to monetize their presence," he said.

However, experts were reporting that the vulnerability of Directors Desk and other online registries highlights the tension between the competitive pressures exchanges NASDAQ is under to offer such services online, and the risk of hacking insider trading.

As we have shown, hackers breaking into NASDAQ's computer systems is nothing new. The execution of trades wasn't compromised, but it remains unclear what other systems were. The hackers didn't tamper with anything, say NASDAQ officials. While Federal investigators, including the Secret Service and the FBI, were independently investigating, there were doubts about the security of the world's stock exchanges, and more doubt whether these web-based services can keep up. The incident is unusual for two reasons.

For one, it proved that even the mightiest organizations have security gaps that cybercriminals can penetrate. Such breaches were made possible, in part, by lax security.

Second, if hackers were trolling around NASDAQ systems and servers for months, and the world heard about it after a breach, we all should have some serious concerns. Further, how was it possible for hackers to breach the system in and out several times without anyone at NASDAQ raising an eyebrow?

In February 2011, the Canadian government confirmed a hack of some of its computer databases. The "unprecedented cyberattack" provided the alleged foreign hackers with access to highly classified federal information.

The Winnipeg Free Press that year reported that Data contained in the federal Finance Department and Treasury Board computers would allow information on private citizens to fall into the hands of hackers.

Increasingly, sophisticated hacking is imperilling personal security, an intrusion into intimate elements of people's lives. Private information is being infiltrated, inspected and manipulated for devious, perverted and unlawful purposes, reports the Winnipeg Free

Press. Virtually no Internet communication information is safe from hackers.

According to the US Federal Bureau of Investigation, hacking activity is increasing at the rate of 30 percent annually.

"Millions of people are participating in globalized hacker culture," an FBI report warned. "It's a highly collaborative industry, usually involving seasoned professionals."

"Being hacked is one of the worst online nightmares because hackers get access to every account you maintain," an official at Symantec's Antispam Engineering told the CNBC news. "A common scenario is that someone hijacks your Webmail account without your knowledge, then pretends to be you and sends emails requesting financial assistance to everyone on your contact list."

"Hackers can send emails as if they are you," explained one Internet security analyst to the same CNBC report, requesting anonymity. "One way is by "spoofing " or "phishing " in which a hacker sends a message that seems to come from you, and a recipient opens it because it appears to come from a trusted source... and this is very common."

The health insurer Anthem announced in 2015 hackers obtained personal information and employment data for members of affiliated health plans reportedly affecting 78.8 million individuals. The incident began with a "phishing" campaign.

Marriott International announced in 2018 that unauthorized access to a database since 2014 resulted in the theft of contact and reservation information for up to 383 million customers, including 9.1 million unique encrypted payment-card numbers and 5.3 million unique unencrypted passport numbers.

The incident began with a "phishing" campaign.

Then, in December of 2018, an employee with "ill-intention" at Desjardins Group collected information about nearly 3 million people and businesses and reportedly leaked it to others outside the Quebec-based financial institution, according to a police special task force.

Public Safety Canada in 2015 defined cyberbullying as "Willful and repeated harm inflicted through the use of computers, cell phones, and other electronic devices."

Cyberbullying incidents intended to threaten, harass, embarrass, or socially exclude another using online technology. As with traditional bullying, there is usually a power imbalance between the cyberbully and the victim.

The most common type of cyberbullying behaviour reported by Canadian adolescents is name-calling. Other, much less common, forms of mean or cruel practice includes harassing someone during an online game, spreading rumours, posting embarrassing photos or videos of someone, making fun of race/religion/ethnicity, a person's sexual orientation, and sexually harassing someone.

A 2018 Pew Research Center survey found that 59 percent of US teens have personally experienced at least one of six types of abusive online behaviours. The most common type of harassment that youth encounter online is name-calling. Some 42 percent of teens report they have been called offensive names online or via their cell phones. The spreading of rumours accounts for 32 percent, while 21 percent report they have been targets of physical threats online. One-quarter of teens say they received explicit images.

These experiences are particularly concerning to parents, with 57 percent of parents reporting they worry about their teen receiving or sending explicit images and posting offensive messages.

Globally, people are feeling uneasy by the viral spread of misinformation on their social media channels. Internet home safety is a grave concern, and the online services we have come to enjoy having a cost – our personal information. Personal data supercharges the use of purchase algorithms, a dysgenic "let's get to know your needs" for a more accessible and a more pleasant online shopping experience.

Parents will need to become savvy when it comes to online safety. We need to end the slapdash attitude of laissez-faire and begin learning about viruses, online privacy, phishing, social networking etiquette, child predators, bullying, and take control of the future.

Richard Tardif
Investigative Journalist, Author and Public Speaker

PART ONE

INTRODUCTION

Social media is the easiest, cheapest and fastest way for today's cybercriminals and scammers to infiltrate home computers and corporate networks. Cybercriminals want to scam you out of your hard-earned money; in many cases, by tricking you into clicking on the links you shouldn't.

As a federal government cleared, International award-winning Certified Ethical Hacker, a Cyologist™ and an Internet Safety lecturer, I will explore in this book what Internet Safety means to you, your family, your employer and your business.

I'm going to teach you how cybercriminals prey on you. I will also show you how to avoid being hacked or scammed.

WHO AM I?

I have an interesting job where I am hired by companies to legally hack into their systems and help find all their vulnerabilities before cybercriminals turn their lives inside out.

My career in Information Technology (IT) began over 20 years ago. In 2001, I got a chance to work as a Premium Support Engineer for a large software company at the time known as Novell. At Novell, I provided escalation network support to some of Canada's largest companies and government entities.

I was inspired by shows like CSI and 24, wondering how characters like Chloe O'Brian were able to hack into network systems so fast. I discovered a course in Washington, D.C., called the Certified Ethical Hacker (CEH). The course offers training in the tools and tactics used by cybercriminals, the very skills I use today by legally hacking into and then securing client networks.

In 2005, my boss at Novell, Jim Yip, found a way to get me into CEH training. During the course, I had the privilege of learning side-by-side with the FBI, CIA and Lockheed Martin employees.

Armed with the knowledge of how to break into corporate networks and computer systems, I felt it was my duty to educate the general public, parents and children on the subject of Internet Safety. I became a member of the High Technology Crime Investigation Association (HTCIA)

It wasn't long before the media began to interview me whenever a data breach occurred. The exposure led to live keynote events in front of thousands and presenting in schools where I get to show the kids how they can be tracked online by what they post, as well as educate the parents on how to keep their kids safe just like they do in the real world.

I began to reflect on the last 20 plus years of my IT life. I have had the opportunity to help companies on the verge of bankruptcy because they've lost all their corporate data. It was my job to help retrieve their data. I've also helped individuals who were being extorted and also helped parents and their kids stay safe online. In January 2011, I left Novell to start my own cybersecurity business.

THE CONCERNS

Are you a busy person? Do you want to help your family and friends remain safe online and keep up with technology? You've read in the media about all these mega hacks and spying all because someone innocently clicked on a link they shouldn't have, letting cybercriminals in through the backdoor and bypassing all the security controls.

Cybercriminals don't want to waste time trying to break through firewalls and other security technologies. Why would they? All they have to do is send you a specially crafted email in reply to something you posted online and then trick you into clicking on a link.

This technique is also being used to trick our kids into hacking each other's online social media accounts, and sending out hateful or sexual content to their friends believing it came from the account holder. The result has led to teen suicide, drug use, severe depression, and there's no stopping this unless parents, teachers and law enforcement pay attention and become involved.

There are many examples, but maybe you've heard of a 14-year-old in Italy jumping to her death after hateful comments about her in 2014 were posted online on a website called Ask.fm?

Ask.fm is a site where you can post an unchecked question, and many people around the world can respond. In this situation, the 14-year-old turned to the web for advice when her boyfriend left her. She received many offensive comments such as "Kill yourself", and "Nobody wants you" and "You aren't normal". When she posted some photographs of her cuts she said she had made on her arms, one commenter wrote, "I hope that one of these days you cut the big vein on your arm and die."

THE GOOD NEWS

Soon, you will become as equally knowledgeable as your children. If you had complete access to up-to-date information on the latest tactics on how to protect yourself, your family and your business from online threats, do you think it would help?

As I mentioned, I have an exciting job where I get paid to legally break into company computer systems and help my clients secure them before the cybercriminals take over. With that experience, I give talks and seminars at school boards, family groups, youth centres, law enforcement, government and companies concerned about protecting themselves online. If there is one thing I have learned, it is that parents, teachers, administrators, council workers, and youth directors feel they can't keep up with their kids when it comes to technology.

I am writing this book for everyone.

Viruses, scams, zombies, botnets, worms, Trojan horses, logic bombs, social engineering, to name a few. How much do you know about these things? Have you ever heard about them? Did you know they're a threat to you every hour of your day?

There's a lot out there, but we can do this!

Why aren't we winning over the cyberbullies, predators and cybercriminals? By reading this book, you're going to learn enough to begin getting a handle on all this overwhelming Internet Safety stuff. You don't have to scour the Internet for the best information on Internet safety, and there is a lot out there, and in this book, you will see that I have your back.

I know what you're thinking?

What's the big picture here? What's the Secret?

The secret is, there are no secrets - just things you don't know yet.

CHAPTER ONE

TAKING THE FIRST STEP

During seminars, I love to ask the audience, "Who knows how to use Google?" Everyone raises their hands. Then I ask, "How many of you "really" know how to use Google?"

There's a reason for the Google question.

TURN ON SAFESEARCH

I'm going to show you a quick trick of how you can limit your searches to specific information that you didn't know existed.

Let's fire up a browser and let's go to www.google.com.

This is where people do their searches, but once you're there, the first thing I want you to do is to go into your settings and change the search settings. You see here; we have "TURN ON SAFESEARCH". SafeSearch means that if there's any content that's not appropriate in your search, it will not appear. Because we want to find information about ourselves, we want to turn Safesearch to no filtering. Then you want to scroll down and save your settings.

In my case, I'm going to type in my name because during a live event, we used someone else's name, and inappropriate content showed up. Needless to say, he was red-faced. If I search for Terry Cutler, I end up with about 619,000 hits.

That's too much information to find out about somebody. Do you know how I can get more specific to this search? Quotation marks. If I put quotes around my name, this will tell Google to "look for what's in between these quotes." Even if it's spelt wrong, it's going to be searching precisely for the subject between quotes. If I hit enter, I'm down to about 26,700 hits.

Let's say you're searching for information about yourself. You want to type something about you that you think might be of public knowledge — for example, occupation or sport. I've seen situations where you might be the soccer dad, and another parent decided to build a website that had your name along with all the other coaches and contact details. The contact number was your private cell phone number.

Because I'm in the cybersecurity business, I'll type in the word "hacker." My hits now drop down to less than 7,300. I'm often in the media, and I don't want to see my website. I only want to see the information that maybe other people are posting about me. Do you know how to remove search results that you don't want to see? Use the minus symbol.

I'm going to go here and start removing search results by typing minus TerryCutler.com. The words Terry Cutler will be removed from the entire list while we continue removing more web pages. We can keep eliminating it. Using the minus sign starts the process of looking for your information online. For example, type in your phone number, what school you belong to, where you work, or any specific personal information you believe is online.

During a live workshop, most didn't find much information. Some children discovered online newspaper photos and information relating to their soccer team, posted by a third party.

Have you ever heard of Google Alerts?

This service monitors the Web for keywords that are of interest to you. If you go to google.com/alerts and press enter, you'll be able to enter a keyword such as your name, your kid's name or anything you choose, and the moment new content is published, and Google becomes aware, it will send you an email with a link to the content.

Here's an example of my Google search string that I use to see what people are posting about me. "terry cutler" hacker -"dr terry cutler" -terrycutler.com -securityweek.com -www.facebook.com/terrypcutler -www.linkedin.com -digitallocksmiths.ca -symantec -"Tips from the Ethical Hacker guy"

CYBERBULLYING

Did you know the psychological and emotional outcomes of cyberbullying are similar to those of real-life bullying? The differences are, real-life bullying often ends when school lets out while cyberbullying, there is no end. And it's getting worse.

More than 43 percent of kids report some form of online bullying. Over 80 percent of teens use a cell phone regularly, making it the most common medium for cyberbullying. More than 70 percent of students report seeing frequent bullying online, and 81 percent of young people think bullying online is easier to get away with than bullying in person.

Types of cyberbullying are: flaming, posting mean messages online in chat rooms or through emails; harassing, repeatedly sending malicious messages; outing, sharing secrets or private pictures or videos; exclusion, intentionally leaving someone out of a group; impersonation, pretending to be someone else to either harass or to find out personal information; and stalking, continuously following a person and harassing them online.

Here is an alarming fact - only one victim in ten will tell a parent or trusted adult of their abuse. I know what you're thinking. The child can quickly delete the account, and it'll all go away.

The truth is the cyberbullying will continue behind the screens, the private pictures leaked, the mocking, the harassment will affect your child's interactions at school and home. I assure you, it's happening.

Laws are being passed to make cyberbullying illegal, but parents I talk with don't even know about cyberbullying. The only way to bridge the digital divide is for parents to become tech-savvy and become familiar with the online world.

Teenagers posting offensive messages on a free social networking site AskFM have reportedly been linked to several suicides. Adolescents who have committed suicide after being hounded by other users on Ask.fm like Rebecca Sedwick, 12, who jumped from the top of a cement factory in Florida in 2015, Hannah Smith, 14, of

England, who hanged herself, and Joshua Unsworth, 15, of England, who hanged himself. How does one prevent online bullying and its horrible consequences?

THE INTERNET AS A BABYSITTER

Technology in the past has served as a babysitter. Television, as one example, is known as being used as a babysitter, and the interaction between children and the TV is passive. They sit down, watch, or change the channel. If a parent is in the kitchen and didn't like what was on TV, they'd walk into the room and change the channel.

Today, with Internet-enabled technologies, it's about the children being active. They can click on sites, enter chats without a parent being the wiser. The parents, in many cases, have fallen behind this technology and are passive – meaning they have no idea how to monitor, safeguard or even keep up with modern Internet technology.

An open and honest relationship between parents and children is one of the best ways to protect from these online risks.

The Camera in Your Computer

Often overlooked is this camera can be a spy camera in the hands of a person. Cybercriminals looking in can learn personal information from background items in a room. For example, the name of a school on a uniform, or a teen's nametag on a sports jersey.

By piecing together a few items in the view of the camera, someone posing as a teen, but much older, could learn a few things about your teen. All someone with mal-intent needs is a few pieces of information to start an investigation.

Differences in Schedules

Sometimes forgotten in parental supervision are the differences in schedules.

While you're asleep, they text and chat, and this accounts for why your teen may be tired at school. They are texting or chatting between 10 p.m. and 4 a.m. That is the best time to take their handheld devices and lock their computers.

Internet cyberbullies are intruding, and it's our job, as parents, to put an end to this.

Public Safety Canada offers the following advice.

Listen to Your Child

Allow him/her to talk about bullying without being judged, criticized or made to feel uncomfortable. By remaining calm and simply listening without over-reacting, the lines of communication are more likely to stay open.

Offer Support and Advocacy

Discuss potential actions with your child and make sure that he/she is comfortable with the action before you proceed. Children stop talking to their parents about their problems. Fearing their parents will embarrass them.

Inform Yourself of the Legal Consequences

Work with your child to keep records of emails, chat room history, web postings or phone messages. These records can be shared with your Internet service provider, the police, and your child's teacher and/or principal.

Validate Your Child's Feelings

Explain that it's normal to feel sad, angry, fearful, frustrated, and lonely. Talking about feelings will help. Value your child's opinion on what could help and what could make things worse.

CHAPTER TWO

PUNCH OUT THE POP-UPS

In chapter one, we explored how to uncover if someone is using your name without your knowledge. I also showed you how to automate that using Google Alerts. Just remember, what I taught you is just the tip of a massive iceberg.

This chapter is about adware, spyware, and how to know if you've been or are being spied on. One question I get asked all the time is, "How do I deal with those in-your-face adware pop-ups that seem to come out of nowhere?"

These flashy, well-designed pop-ups look professional and legitimate. As good as they appear, pop-ups are infected with software programmed to lift your credit card and banking information, and that means they're after your identity.

These threats are designed to hold your data hostage. The only way to get it back is to pay cybercriminals anywhere between $500-$25,000, an extortion tactic known as ransomware, which we'll cover in the next chapter.

Learning how to avoid threats will be invaluable in defending against becoming the next victim.

How do we avoid and get rid of adware? I make it a point to check out a PC every once in a while, and you guessed it, the PC owners were victims, unknowingly, of adware.

ADWARE

Adware is an advertisement that appears on the web or in software, aptly named Adware. In many cases, adware accompanies a program you downloaded.

You install the software and keep clicking "NEXT, NEXT, NEXT and INSTALL," not realizing that the installing software said it was going to introduce some ad toolbars into your browser. It's easy for cybercriminals to inject infected ads into the ad network, and that's part of the reason why you're getting pop-ups.

As an example, while visiting a legitimate website, did you spot a pop-up that says, "Your PC is infected and running slow, boost it now with this antivirus solution?" These fake software programs could damage your computer or worse, give someone else control of your computer.

The adware sends you an installation notification that some advertising programs are installing. The catch? To use the new software, you will see some ads from time to time. Some freeware that may contain adware are:

- Advanced search engines
- Instant news and weather updates
- Computer games
- Peer-to-peer (P2P) file-sharing programs
- Fun mouse pointers, desktop themes and backgrounds
- Emoticons and smileys used in email
- Applications that say they will improve efficiency

Then there are the ads that promise to make your life easier with a new search engine. You can compare prices between hotels or choose from twenty styles of clothes and then compare the prices.

Sounds great, and away we go, clicking, and then we click "NEXT" or "MORE", but now is the time to pull back on the reins.

Is it too good to be true?

Of course, we would love the world at our fingertips, but as we move further along the continuous CLICK, make sure you look carefully at the ask. "In exchange for offering you free software products, we collect anonymous usage information from your computer."

This question continues. "Our partners and this company may use this information to select and display targeted branded pop-ups." If you go ahead with your CLICKS and accept, not only will your workflow be interrupted by these annoying pop-ups; but in the background, someone, something, is packing data, your data on your shopping habits, your browsing habits, your email address, and your sensitive information. This data could end up in the hands of unscrupulous advertisers, or cybercriminals.

You may have uninstalled these applications from your computer, but there are still little nuggets left behind tracking your browsing habits.

Now the ads are appearing in your inbox with clickable links. How convenient? I think you know what happens when you click on the wrong link, right? You get hacked.

Customarily, the criminals install a backdoor where they can enter and leave as they please. They can turn on your webcam, record you and your family, or listen to private conversations.

Cybercriminals can now copy your files to a remote location. Tax information, your CV, medical records, and scanned documents such as void cheques, digital signatures, or passports, are in the hands of...well, not in your hands.

Further, you may have sexual images and videos of you and your significant other on your PC. That's when sextortion comes into play.

IS MY PC HACKED?

Here are a few questions I get asked several times a week.

"How do I know if someone hacked my PC?"

"How do I know if someone is spying on me through my webcam?"

A simple command-line tool can provide invaluable information about what's happening on your system to find out if your PC has been taken over by a cybercriminal or malware.

This is a complex topic to explain in a book; I have a live demonstration available at www.InternetSafetyUniversity.com

If you prefer, you can read below.

The first thing you want to do is close as many open programs as you can, like Microsoft Outlook, Skype, etc. Closing programs will allow us to find unwanted communications to your PC from unknown applications.

Next, press the "START" button, and type CMD, which is short for command prompt and press "ENTER".

Once the command prompt is open, type NETSTAT (space) –ANO.

What we're doing here is asking windows to list all listening and open ports in the system. The state of the connection can be listening or an established communication. We are looking for established communication. Established communication means your computer is communicating with another network device somewhere on the Internet.

Next, open the windows task manager by right-clicking on the taskbar and select "START TASK MANAGER". You can also get there by pressing "CTRL-ALT-DELETE" and choosing "TASK MANAGER". Once it's open, click on the "PROCESSES TAB". Select "VIEW" at the top, and choose "SELECT COLUMNS". You'll notice that PID is unchecked. Please go ahead and check that box. A PID (process identifier) is the name of the software that's talking on this connection. We'll use a PID to investigate.

Some of you have Windows 10, and it's not the same way to enable this function. In Windows 10, make sure you right-click on the bottom toolbar and choose "TASK MANAGER" Once the task manager is open, click on the "DETAILS TAB" and then right-click on the "NAME" in the column and choose "SELECT COLUMN". Once the choices show up, put a checkbox in the PID box.

You'll notice that some numbers show up beside the names of the processes. For simplicity reasons, you'll need to click to sort the process ID from smallest to largest, so we can find stuff quickly. You'll also notice a button called "SHOW PROCESSES FROM ALL USERS". Let's make sure we press that as well so we can see every communication with your PC.

Now, what you would do is match up the process numbers with the name of the application. For example, process Id 4668 is running twice. What could this be? Once we get to 4668, we can see that Skype (or on your computer another application) is using this ID, which is most likely safe. Continue going through this list, and if there's something you're not sure about, Google is your friend at this point. You could also right-click and select "PROPERTIES". Properties might give you a little more insight into the type of program, and the location of the file.

If you're still running into trouble, you'll need to contact your family IT guy or bring it into a Best Buy for servicing.

I invite you to join the 1000 plus members on our InternetSafetyUniversity Facebook page, where we can share ideas. You never know if your question will be a feature in an upcoming video.

CHAPTER THREE

RANSOMWARE AND 6.4 QUADRILLION YEARS

Ransomware is the latest form of online extortion targeting businesses and individuals. Ransomware is becoming far more advanced, as was evident in 2017 when a global cyberattack spread the ransomware to 150 countries.

Imagine you're the CEO of the company and you show up to work and find out that all your corporate data is encrypted, unusable, and no employees can work. You also learn that the data backups are also encrypted and unusable. Also, your sensitive data is now up for ransom. To have your data returned, you'll have to pay big bucks.

What do you do now?

On every computer screen is a message; "Unfortunately, the files on this computer have been encrypted. You have 72 hours to submit a payment of $500 to receive the encryption key; otherwise, the price will go up every hour after that. After 72 hours, your files will be permanently destroyed."

Payment must be in bitcoin currency.

Bitcoin? What on earth is Bitcoin? We'll talk more about that a little later.

You ignore the message and try to access your photos, family videos, corporate and personal documents, accounting files. That's when you notice that all the files have been renamed and encrypted and are unusable.

You realize now that your computer is under attack, and your last known data backup was eight months ago.

What do you do now?

You might try to rename your files back or call your IT specialist to come and help you. Let me save you some trouble. You're wasting your time, and there's no way out. Your data is now encrypted with military-grade 2048-bit encryption, and according to Digicert.com, it would take the average desktop computer about 6.4 quadrillion years to crack the code. Your computer is under a ransomware attack. Ransomware is a form of online extortion targeting both businesses and individuals.

To make matters worse, ransomware is designed to track down your backups and encrypt them also. Cybercriminals will do anything they can to get your money.

Unfortunately, once your files are encrypted, there's not much you can do besides cut your losses or pay up. Even the FBI says there's no way out of it and to pay the ransom. If you do pay up, there's a chance you won't get your files back, so you're out the data and your cash.

You might be asking yourself, how is this crime happening, and why aren't the malicious hackers arrested?

There are several parts to this answer.

Most of this crime originates in third-world countries that have a low monthly average income of $600. Anyone in a third-world country, to generate more income, can buy a ransomware kit and then land a victim, scamming them out of $500. Multiply this by ten victims, and the extortionists can potentially rack in anywhere from $3,000 to $10,000 a month.

As a victim, it doesn't make sense to spend thousands of dollars on investigators and lawyers to get back extorted $500. Further, law enforcement will simply take your complaint. Unless, the extortion is significant, as in more than $500 thousand, you're on your own. That's why not much is changing.

HOW RANSOMWARE WORKS

You open an email with an attached ZIP file. Maybe you clicked a link or on an infected pop-up advertisement? Perhaps you visited an infected website? Ransomware can even come in the form of an attached Word document or PDF.

While surfing the Web, you see the message "Your computer is running slow, optimize it now with this antivirus software." You think, "I could use a speed boost on my computer." Without further thought, you download and install. Now, the bad guys are holding your computer and data hostage and are attempting to extort a ransom payment.

Today, ransomware has become so sophisticated. This malicious software can detect data on your local computer and any external USB hard drive.

Once in your network, it can detect other computers in your system and infect it remotely without any user interaction. When ransomware is running wild inside a business, they can be offline for 60-100 hours, and in some cases, there's no data recovery. The company may shut its doors.

One attack, dubbed "WannaCry" was indiscriminately spreading like wildfire not only inside corporations but also at the home user level. For many, infections like WannaCry, and others like RYUK, and Bad Rabbit are a wake-up call about the threat ransomware poses today and user lack of preparedness. About four in 10 companies have a strategy to deal with this destructive software.

Cybercriminals often ask for a nominal payment, figuring you'll be more likely to pay to avoid the hassle and heartache of dealing with the virus. They may ask for as little as $300 to be paid through an untraceable currency called bitcoin.

Ransomware threats earned cybercriminals over an estimated $1 billion in 2014 and rose to $8 billion in 2018. Global cybercrime will reach $6 trillion by 2021.

Even though ransomware has existed for a while, it has exploded in recent years because of four primary drivers:
1. There're more distribution channels
2. It's cheaper to build and comes with 24/7 support from criminals
3. Increasingly lucrative targets
4. Bitcoin and other untraceable digital currencies

Bitcoins are a form of digital cryptocurrency and don't have a physical representation. Instead, they are stored in an online exchange in anonymous virtual wallets. Bitcoins can be transferred anywhere, with anonymity. They are an ideal form of payment for illicit activities and to cybercriminals.

The price of one bitcoin had a value of $100-$200 back in 2013, but as of January 2, 2020, one bitcoin is worth USD $7,321. It is believed that 17.7 million bitcoins are available. With all the anonymity, it's no wonder cryptocurrency is one of the enabling factors of ransomware.

If cybercriminals couldn't accept payment safely, then the malicious software would have no value. Unfortunately, with the rise of Bitcoin, comes the increase in ransomware. Bitcoin is untraceable, providing an anonymous, friction-free way to transact private commerce.

Demanding payment in Bitcoin, cybercriminals expect anonymity, which makes collecting ransoms easy, because the transaction also bypasses a banks' anti-fraud measures.

TOR ANONYMITY NETWORK

The last piece of this puzzle for cybercriminals is to get on to the TOR Anonymity Network

TOR stands for "The Onion Router" and is a well-crafted network and browser developed to enhance and anonymize Internet traffic. TOR uses a particular browser configured to use a worldwide volunteer network of relays. All traffic is encrypted. The network was designed from the ground up to anonymize and hide the source and destination traffic.

TOR networks are used to communicate or host websites that cannot be easily tracked by law enforcement or government officials. It can also be a tool for circumventing censorship, but also a tool for more nefarious use of anonymous traffic.

Ahead we will look at what to do before a ransomware attack.

BEFORE A RANSOMWARE ATTACK

In today's world, everyone is cyber-attacked, so it comes down to two types of people — those who are already hacked, and those that don't know it yet. There's no silver bullet to stop a hacker. There are ways to make it difficult for cybercriminals to penetrate your network.

Back-up and Restore: The most critical and essential part of any ransomware security strategy is regular daily data backups. Most companies do this, but surprisingly few run backups and restore drills. Home users? Unlikely. Both processes are important. You should run a restore test at least once a week because it's the only way to know ahead of time whether your backup plan is working. Because you never know, right? You may have some kinks to work through before crisis mode hits. With regular backups and restore testing, the devastation of a ransomware attack will have less impact, compared to what could happen if no backups are performed.

Here's a tip:

If you back up your files to an external hard drive or an online backup service, you'll diminish the chances of losing all your data. Also, it's essential to enable encryption on your back-up as well.

Here's a problem you'll face with an attached USB external drive. Ransomware is designed to attack the files on your PC and all its connections. If you're at work connected to the network or have your external USB drive plugged in, the ransomware is designed to go after it all. Which means your back-ups will be lost? Make sure the external drive is disconnected following every backup.

For home users, install a network hard drive at another location other than your home and that your PC has to log in and copy the data over, and disconnects on its own after the copy. It's a great option if you have an unlimited data plan; this way, if you get hit, you can just format your PC, reinstall the OS and restore your data like nothing happened.

Update and Patch: Next, you'll want to ensure your operating systems, security software and patches are up to date for all devices. It sounds basic enough, but according to a recent survey, about half of IT professionals admit they struggle to keep up with the sheer volume of patches released every week.

Teams also struggle when updating specific applications, like Adobe Flash, because it might break other compatibilities relying on the software. Hackers understand that IT departments can't mass update all the systems. Once a patch comes out because it can break functionality on the network. Cybercriminals use that window of time.

New ransomware can scan your network and find unpatched systems and infect it on its own without any user intervention. Even if you patched 99.999 percent of your network and that one server that was used to test software didn't have the latest patches, that ransomware can exploit it, steal the administrator password from its memory, and then log in and encrypt the other 99 percent.

That's terrifying, isn't it?

Train and Educate, Beware of Macros: Awareness training is critical to combating ransomware.

Again, most ransomware infections begin with a single well-intentioned employee opening a work-related email. Once the application opens, it can bankrupt a company overnight. Research shows that cybercriminals actively exploit human error by triggering a sense of urgency and curiosity. In 2019, 300 people were let go by an Arkansas company when The Heritage Company was hit with ransomware, unable to maintain operations and eventually closing their doors: even after paying the ransom.

These attacks play on the user's lack of awareness and typically require them to open various malicious files such as Word document attachments, PDFs or ZIP files.

Sometimes you might receive a file, for example, that says "account_statement.txt.doc."

You need to understand that this is not a text file, it's a word doc file. File Extensions are the last three letters of a filename after the period. The reason this is important is when it comes to ransomware your computer is set up to hide file extensions of known types.

Going back to my "account_statement.txt.doc" file example, often, your email will show the file extension, but when you download the file, you may not see the extension. The "account_statement.txt.doc" file is actually " "account_statement.doc."

There are other ways for a cybercriminal to get around this.

They may include a Zip file called "fedex.zip" that contains multiple files inside with altered extensions. Your email program only sees a Zip file, but in reality, the Zip file contains a single file called "fedex.xls.exe."

The latest ransomware is extremely hard to detect and is well designed. Worse part is, the executable .exe files are not the only dangerous type of files out there. You might see files with extensions such as .bat, .cmd, .com, .lnk, .pif, .scr, .vb, .vbe, .vbs, .wsh, and .jar.

Robust emails, Mobile & Social Media Security Solutions: Most ransomware slips in through email, mobile devices and social media. You need to have advanced solutions that can stop these threats in real-time.

You need to stay away from free antivirus solutions and free Malwarebytes. The paid versions have real-time protection and artificial intelligence that can help protect you.

Older traditional legacy mail gateways, web filters, and antivirus software should also be updated to the latest technology and running on all networks. If not, you won't be able to stop the latest threats. Today's antivirus solutions analyze every website you visit and every email attachment you receive to ensure that no malicious content breaches the system.

Cybercriminals are always one step ahead. Actually, it feels like 12 steps, but who's counting, and typical email security configurations rely far too heavily on outdated signatures. Remember what I said earlier? Virus scanners are signature-based technology, which means it has to update itself every few hours to keep up with the latest viruses. If you don't have the virus scanner that recognizes threats and lets them through, you'll be infected.

In the future, virus protection on our mobile devices will be routine. Imagine waking up one morning to turn on your phone, and you have a ransom note telling you to pay up?

WHAT TO DO DURING A RANSOMWARE ATTACK

Let's discuss what to do during a ransomware attack. When I speak at conferences and talk about ransomware, the common question I get asked is, "How do I know if I'm infected?" How does infection occur?

On your desktop, you usually have documents ranging from videos, word documents, and PDFs. When you open a file, you'd be able to see the contents. Now, imagine receiving an unknowingly malicious file in your email, and then you open it. You then notice all these new files, and your desktop and your background image just changed to a ransom note.

At this point, your heart is in your throat. You're starting to sweat, and start having flashbacks about if you did do that backup, and if it worked.

If you look at the ransom note, it says, "oops your important files are encrypted" and to look for a decrypter file to begin the process of getting your data back. Now, you'll notice a pop-up window with a countdown timer to when you'd have to pay the ransom before they destroy the key.

At that point, there is no way to get your data back. If you try to open up a regular text file, windows don't recognize the extension anymore. If you decide to open it with a notepad, you will see the document encrypted with WannaCry. It's completely unreadable and unusable.

You'll also notice that it copies an image file to your desktop, which matches the background. There's also a text file that has instructions on how to get your data back.

Your next question? "How can I trust you?"

"We'll decrypt your files for sure because no one will trust us if we cheat users." Like seriously? How reassuring Mr. Criminal.

There's even a "contact us" button where you can interact with the bad guys in case you need tech support to pay the bill. In my example, which was a real ransomware attack, they're asking for $300 worth of bitcoin. Most individuals and small businesses that get hit with ransomware don't have a clue about bitcoins.

If you receive a ransomware demand like this, you need to report it immediately to your security team and law enforcement—and never try to pay this ransom on your own. Making a payment may damage a company's brand reputation and security ramifications if not done correctly.

DISCONNECT FROM THE NETWORK

The moment you detect a ransomware demand or notice something odd, such as suddenly losing access to your files, disconnect from the network by pulling the network cable out from behind the computer, or by unplugging from your Wi-Fi.

If you don't unplug from the Wi-Fi network, your computer will begin encrypting all the files and the corporate server. Encryption will create outages and no access for co-workers because the files are all encrypted. The ransomware is already scanning for other computers on the network that don't have all the Windows updates installed.

After disconnecting from the network, you must unplug any storage devices such as USB or external hard drives connected to your computer. If you don't, the ransomware will encrypt all the essential files on those external hard drives. Don't bother trying to erase anything or try to "clean up" any files with antivirus software because I promise you; you're wasting your time.

You won't be able to decrypt the new ransomware viruses. Focus on unplugging the computer from the network and any other storage devices.

Next, make sure you notify the IT department that your computer has been infected and then hand it over. They may not be able to do anything, but they'll at least begin to reinstall.

Having this "prevent" knowledge is like knowing how to put out a grease fire at home.

Most people would throw water on a grease fire, which would make it worse. You know to use baking soda and a non-glass pan lid. See what I mean?

LAW ENFORCEMENT

Ransomware is a crime because data theft and extortion are in play. Nobody has the right to seize devices, networks or data, let alone demand a ransom. Notifying the proper authorities is a necessary step. Visit your closest police station or don't be afraid to pick up your phone and have them open an investigation, at least for your insurance company. The police are there to help you, but keep in mind there's nothing they can do to help once you're infected.

FREE RANSOMWARE DECRYPTION TOOLS

Some security vendors offer free ransomware decryption programs, and in some rare instances, they can help you retrieve your data without paying the ransom. But most decrypters work for older strains of ransomware or even a single attack campaign. Attackers regularly update their ransomware on a weekly basis. Free tools fall out of date, and likely won't work against a ransomware attack.

You might get lucky with a free decryption tool, but don't make it part of your incident response plan.

It's important to be aware of the payment deadline you're facing, and whether or not paying the ransom is an option? If paying the ransom is out of the question, then you will be free to spend more time delving into the other possible solutions. If you are desperate like most companies, then priority will need to be given to what results you can get in the shortest time-frame.

One tip is to back up the encrypted files. I know you're probably asking, "Why would I do that?"

Malware researchers and computer security experts will sometimes uncover the encryption keys used in ransomware programs. Uncovering might take up to a year, but it has happened. It's a long shot, but you might get lucky down the road.

Now you're sitting there helplessly looking at that time and asking yourself, "Is my data worth paying a ransom?"

We need to assess the scope of the damage.

Some attacks are worse than others. Your response to some of the following questions could determine if you pay the ransom or not. What is the type of attack?

If it's ransomware, then what type is it?

Will free decryption tools be helpful?

Who in your network is compromised?

Is the server's data encrypted as well?

What network permissions do any compromised accounts have? If it's the IT administrator's computer, they usually have access to everything, which could also mean, everything is encrypted.

Time and manpower getting back online. Most ransomware attacks take over 100 hours of recovery time. Paying an IT guy at $100 an hour might be more expensive than paying the ransom. A company also has employees who are unable to work and are still getting paid. You might be the president of a company and have responsibilities to shareholders to keep the business up and running.

RESTORE FROM BACKUP

The only way to completely recover from a ransomware infection is by formatting your computer, reinstalling all the software and restoring all your data from backup…from scratch.

In some cases, with large enterprises, even with recent backups, paying the ransom might make more financial and operational sense. Restoring backups takes time and effort, and most businesses might not be able to afford the downtime. It's a known fact that it can take at least 100 hours to recover from a ransomware attack.

NEGOTIATE AND/OR PAY THE RANSOM?

Let's get down to the money question.

If you have exhausted all other options, and you must have your files back, your only solution might be to pay the ransom. Antivirus and security experts recommend avoiding paying the ransom.

In some cases, you pay the ransom, and you never get your files. In other cases, you pay the payment, get your data back, and then get hit again.

But when you're under the gun of a ransomware threat, you don't have the luxury of time to weigh your moral compass carefully. The attack is here and now.

You can sometimes negotiate a lower price by using the "contact us" link in the ransom pop-up.

Keep in mind that if you do pay up, what you'd be doing is actively funding the attacker who has broken into your network and stolen your data.

It marks you as someone with a vulnerable network and incentive to pay, and it enables the cybercriminal to bankroll future attacks.

No individual or organization wants to be extorted, let alone fund criminal rings.

AFTER THE RANSOMWARE ATTACK

Can you imagine the chaos that unfolds during a ransomware attack? Cybercriminals aren't hacking through firewalls. They are sending crafty and deceiving emails to unsuspecting users. Whether you are an individual, or small business, or a multinational corporation, protecting your network is a vital part of a network security framework.

Regardless of the damage, an attack would reveal security failures somewhere in the chain, whether it be human error or not, which resulted in a device or network compromise. Now that things are back to normal, you have an opportunity to learn from the security breach and avoid future attacks.

One of the things I recommend is a top-to-bottom security assessment, preferably by an outside vendor.

"Why Terry, I have my own IT staff to do it, why spend more money?"

Ethical hackers provide fresh eyes on your environment and might spot weaknesses that your IT staff didn't think of or didn't know. Some ransomware contains other threats or backdoor Trojans that can lead to future attacks. That's why wiping every device and restoring from a clean backup is a must. Now you know why it takes at least 100 hours to recover from a ransomware attack.

One of the tasks I perform during an intrusion test is social engineering.

It's the psychological manipulation of people basically, and I try to fool them into clicking on my non-malicious links so that I can see who needs training.

Another reason why I do this is that most new strains of ransomware rely on human interaction to deploy the virus, which is also known as a payload. If your current security measures fail and an infected and malicious "unpaid invoice" makes its way through your email server, well guess what? Only a well-informed employee will be the last line of defence for a company, hospital or school staying online or becoming another ransomware statistic. We're known as "the human firewall," ensuring that everyone, senior management, employees, staff or faculty are up to date with awareness training.

Invest in an ethical hacking firm to perform an intrusion test. Our mission involves increasing employee awareness and improving company security. We can replicate real-world attacks such as phishing, social engineering and social media exploits. Ethical hackers can analyze and identify security vulnerabilities ahead of actual attacks.

INVEST IN MODERN DEFENCES

Most firewalls and antivirus are decent at blocking known threats, but that's not good enough for today's fast-changing security landscape. Security requires solutions that can analyze, identify and prevent malicious links and attachments, and it has to occur in real-time.

The free antivirus or free Malwarebytes that you might be using just won't cut it. You're missing out on all the real-time protection capabilities required to keep up with new threats. Think about it? One user's interaction with the ransomware initiates or allows a network intrusion.

Only after a user has accidentally clicked or visited a malicious link will your secondary lines of defences kick in. In the first line of defence, you will need to harden the human sitting at the keyboard.

THE HUMAN BEHIND THE COMPUTER

People don't come to work to click on phishing emails and infect their computers and company systems. That's why employees need training to spot the red flags so that they can differentiate between a legitimate and malicious link.

The methods of attacks are continually changing. It's vital to keep users up-to-date on the basics of IT and email security, but also the ever-changing purpose of attacks.

But what if "Francesca" from the "accounting department" accidentally emails you an excel file called "corporate payroll?" Not everyone is going to check to see if this email is legit or just a well-crafted phishing email, especially with a juicy attachment like corporate payroll.zip. HR is another target. They may receive 15 resumes a day, but only one of those needs to be malicious to cause an incident.

Education is key.

CHAPTER FOUR

USB KEYS IN THE URINAL

Why do cybercriminals choose you? You shouldn't take it personally. Cybercriminals create a software script that goes out to the Internet searching for specific versions of any vulnerable software. What cybercriminals know too well, is that people love to click on the links in their emails. The more clicks, meaning more visitors embedded in the cybercriminal list, the more crime they can potentially commit using your infected computer.

We call the unsuspecting link clickers, the "Clicky Clicky People," and if you happen to be on that list because you haven't stayed up to date with the software, you're about to have a bad day.

If you own a website, it's critical that you stay current with software updates as they're released. You might be asking, "Why would someone want to target my website, or my home computer if there's no value?" The goal for any cybercriminal is to steal traffic from your website by injecting code and embedding links that will infect your visitors, too.

As an example, someone, including yourself, could visit a website, and when you get to the home page, you notice that a PDF file is automatically downloading to your computer. You think, "What could this be?" You open it, and you see the screen flicker a few times then, you're done. Now, you realize that you didn't install all those pesky Adobe updates you were warned about for the last few months, and the virus took advantage of the software flaws that made it vulnerable.

The biggest challenge we have in IT security today is that people won't care until it's too late. You need to remember that cybercriminals have automated tools that scan for systems that still have the default settings from the time you purchased the product, with the same default password. Have you seen the news reports about people wondering how their baby monitors are being taken over and being spied on via your IP camera system or smart home?

IS THE INTERNET CURSED?

Some say the Internet is cursed. Viruses, scams, zombies, botnets, worms, Trojan horses, logic bombs, social engineering, just to name a few. Have you heard about them? Did you know they're a threat to you every hour of your day? Let me give you an overview?

A virus is an infection that tries to spread itself to other computers in your home or corporate network. If it finds a vulnerable computer, it'll infect it, and the cycle repeats.

A worm is a little more sophisticated but is a subclass of a virus. A worm is malicious software that will penetrate an operating system and replicate itself to it by relying on security failures. The danger with worms is that it will use the infected Computer to not only send out that one worm, but it could also send out thousands.

The name Trojan horse I'm sure reminds you of the ancient story of the Greeks hiding a bunch of elite soldiers inside a wooden horse, which then attacked when the enemy slept. Similarly, someone will send you software that appears legit and comes from a legitimate source, but the Trojan horse appears once you've finished installing the software.

Logic bombs can be deadly. A logic bomb is a piece of software code that has been intentionally inserted into a software system and will set off once certain conditions are met, like a specific time and date. Have you ever seen the movie Live Free or Die Hard? In the movie, cybercriminals broke into several critical infrastructures throughout the city, and on a certain day, the malicious software turned on and crashed the system. This is an example of a logic bomb. I can see this being the next terrorist attack.

Rootkits are dangerous. Rootkits are designed to stay hidden in an operating system and often disguise themselves as legitimate vital operating system processes; this way, the antivirus won't pick them up. Also, a cybercriminal can get back into the compromised system at any point through the rootkit.

Botnets and zombies work hand in hand. A zombie is a computer that's been infected and compromised and is now a mindless zombie slave to the botnet system. Once your computer is part of a botnet, your computer can be used by cybercriminals to commit crimes. Law enforcement can show up at your door saying you committed a computer crime when, in fact, you didn't.

Social engineering. This is my favourite way of breaking into corporate networks when I get hired…legally. Social engineering is a successful way of playing on people's trust and the desire to help others and tricking them into divulging confidential information that would later be used in a computer attack. Let me give you a real-life example.

THE USB KEYS IN THE URINAL

I was hired by a manufacturing firm in 2011 to try and expose any security vulnerabilities that might be lurking in their network. A company's external infrastructure, including Web servers, Domain Name Servers, email servers, VPN access points, perimeter firewalls, and any other applications publicly accessible from the Internet, is typically considered the primary target of security attacks.

That's where we start.

Our methods include cracking passwords and eavesdropping as well as using keystroke loggers, sniffers, Denial of Service, and remote controls.

In this case, I tried attacking the firewall systems with every trick in my picker's toolkit. Their network was locked tight.

I told myself, "I'm going in."

Companies that have an impenetrable wall against external attacks are often surprisingly open to insider threats. Cybercriminals can expose these vulnerabilities by exploiting a straightforward fact: Most people will respond in a highly predictable way to a particular situation.

been fired off to security managers long before any proprietary data was accessed.

While it's true that security threats are more menacing, remember that security defences have become more powerful. Ensure you take the necessary steps to protect your infrastructure and your data.

WHEN THEY GIVE ME THE KEYS?

Here's another intrusion test I did this time on a retail company.

I walked into one of their outlets, and straight to the employee stocking the shelves and said, "Hi I'm from the IT department, and we're doing an upgrade on the network, can you show me and let me into the server room in the back?" We went to the back to make sure I was in the right place and told the guy, "I'm going to go for lunch, but I'll return with my colleagues, and we'll finish the job."

I returned with two other ethical hacker colleagues and met the same employee. The employee gave me the key without verifying any ID or asking who I work for. We took over the entire lunchroom. The employees didn't have any room to eat because our equipment was everywhere. Not one person asked us who we were. We snapped a selfie and sent it to the IT Director. Think about it? They just gave me the key without verifying my credentials.

Employees are a huge threat to any organization. In many cases, employees are the ones who think they are underpaid and overworked and are unhappy with senior management. If we look at some of the latest data breaches, many of them were at the hands of former employees.

These are the folks who have probably been given too much access and like to poke around the system. They can then use this information for their personal gain.

This is known as an insider threat. There are many misconfigurations when I run an audit and find a list of users who left their company over a year or more ago. These former employees still had access.

Keeping up with outdated software has always been a challenge for IT. Whenever I get hired to perform an intrusion test on companies, I still see Windows XP or Windows 7 being used because the software that controls the security of the doors at the office might not run on later software. The company is stuck with outdated and unsupported operating systems.

And finally, stolen passwords? This is a huge problem now because of extortion. If the scammers can crack your password, they'll email you using the email associated with that account saying, "Hey, you don't know me, but your password is this, we have access to your system etc." And you're sitting there freaking out wondering how they guessed your password.

Let's briefly review three companies that were breached.

First, Under Armour's nutrition App MyFitnessPal was breached in 2018, impacting the information of roughly 150 million users. The intrusion exposed usernames, email addresses, and passwords, indicating systems were at least segmented enough to protect birthdays, location information, or credit card numbers.

Second, Russian cybercriminals in 2012 got into LinkedIn, Dropbox and Formspring, and scooped up data of over 100 million people, including passwords and emails. Phishing campaigns began immediately asking people to change their passwords but using fake or infected links.

Yevgeniy Nikulin was the man accused of hacking computers belonging to the San Francisco-based companies and stealing user names, email addresses and passwords. He was arrested in 2014 and eventually extradited to the US in 2017. Prosecutors say Nikulin, now in his early 30s, used a LinkedIn employee's credentials to access the company's computers in 2012. Nikulin then conspired to sell stolen usernames, passwords and email addresses of Formspring customers.

Third, hospitality giant Marriott in 2018 was hit by a massive hack leading to the theft of personal data of a whopping 500 million customers of its Starwood hotels. A massive breach of Marriott guest data that was thought to have affected around 500 million people, but also exposed the passport numbers of several million people.

The target was its Starwood reservation system and the personal information of hundreds of millions of guests who had stayed at the hotels since 2014.

In case you're thinking, "Why do I care?" The Marriot hack was one of the biggest on record. Marriot owns properties like the W Hotels, the St. Regis, Sheraton Hotels & Resorts, Westin Hotels & Resorts, Element Hotels, Aloft Hotels, The Luxury Collection, Tribute Portfolio, Le Méridien Hotels & Resorts, Four Points by Sheraton, Design Hotels, and Starwood-branded timeshares.

Marriott is by no means the first big company to get hacked. eBay. Target. Home Depot. Chipotle. Equifax. Do you know what these companies have in common? They were all breached. Each company lost data. They have no idea who did it.

Why should you care that your password was stolen?

TIME TO STRENGTHEN YOUR PASSWORDS

Forgetting your password can be a serious hassle; you need to verify your account, remember your high school teacher's pet's middle name, and patiently wait up to a week to unlock said account (looking at you, Apple ID gatekeepers). Given the rise in data breaches—with 22 million records exposed in 2019 alone — to have a strong password both for your protection and privacy. Here's how to create the right password.

There are several types of passwords, including letters, numbers only, and those with special characters. To create a nearly unbreakable password, you want at least 16 to 25 characters, with a combination of letters, numbers and special characters.

As an example, let's create a strong password out of the phrase, "I had a great day at work 2020!" First, remove the spacing and capitalize each letter of each word. Now the password looks like "IHadAGreatDayAtWork2020!" Next, replace the O's with zeros and the A's with @ signs. It'll look something like

"IH@d@Gre@tD@y@tW0rk2020!" This password would take 39 centuries to crack.

The benefit of creating your password instead of using an auto-generated one is that it holds personal meaning to you, so it'll be easier to remember.

Some experts say to create passwords like Gzz4655!!v662@, and others will tell you to create memorable, strong passwords. Both methods are correct for the time being because it requires way too much computing power and time to crack these passwords. But as computer technology becomes faster, this will need to be revisited.

Dangers of Autofill

The Autofill extension serves one purpose: fill form fields automatically on page load without any user interaction. Sure, typing in your username and having the browser auto-populate your saved password is easier, but that's a security death sentence waiting to happen. Autofill grants immediate access to your accounts in the event that someone has confiscated your device.

To prevent you from caving into the autofill trap, the new Google Chrome browser saves you from using the same password for every website. Your securely stored password can be synchronized across multiple devices.

Security Questions

Behind every strong password is a batch of even stronger security questions. But given the prevalence of seemingly harmless memes that request basic information about you, you might be divulging far more information than you intended.

Steer clear of responding to any posts that, under the guise of generating a fun new name, request, for example, your pet's name and the street where you were born.

In that vein, you want to create your own security questions that only you would know the answer to, as opposed to using their default questions.

TWO-STEP VERIFICATION

Two-step verification or authentication adds another layer of security to even the strongest of passwords. How it works is that you'll log into your account with your username and password. The website or social media platform will send a unique code to your mobile device, or you'll use an authenticator app to provide a code. You will then need to input it into the desktop or mobile version of the website. Only then may you begin using the service.

If you ever worked for a big company back in the early '90s, you used to carry a little RSA token around with you where the numbers on it used to change every 30 seconds. This is the same concept, except we're using your mobile phone.

Two-step verification is usually an optional feature that's integral to your security. This advanced security feature should be mandatory and enabled by default on all our online accounts, especially in today's world, where digital crime and Internet fraud is on the rise. When it comes to protecting your data, try to carve out a little space in your brain specifically reserved for password memory.

YOU'VE ALREADY BEEN BREACHED

No longer is it a question of will you be breached, but when? I can go further and say that you've probably been breached already. Just look at the numbers: More than 95 percent of large companies are targeted by malicious traffic. The average cost of each breach is $6-Million and can take up to 45 days to resolve a cyber-attack.

I've witnessed just how fast this number can rise with a client of mine. When a company is breached or hit, you need to involve lawyers; incident response companies that start at $75,000; you also will have your own IT staff working around the clock.

You are obliged to perform a compromise assessment for your cyber insurance company, or wait; you don't have cyber insurance? Better look into that for your business ASAP. As one example, one of my clients saw their bill rise to $1.6-Million in less than 30 days. Had they not had cyber insurance, the breach would have meant financial disaster. When a breach occurs, the majority of information is lost in a matter of hours, not days.

Here's a list of the biggest companies that were breached and lost our personal and sensitive data in 2015. Target, vTech, F.B.I., Trump Hotels, Patreon, Experian, Scottrade, Ashley Madison, Excellus BlueCross BlueShield, CVS/Walgreens, UCLA Health, OPM, LastPass, IRS, and Anthem, just to mention the few.

You would think that companies would dedicate more resources and implement new processes to protect customer personal information and cardholder data before and after a breach?

Unfortunately, many company boards of directors believe that they will never experience a breach and, as such, do not put adequate resources to protect our information. I like to tell those boards of directors, "IT security is the last thing you think about until it's the only thing you think about." A data breach will damage a company's reputation, which will cause its customers to lose trust in the brand, all of which will have a negative impact on the marketplace. It will also create financial losses for the shareholders if class action lawsuits are filed for negligence. The most victimized will be the unsuspecting customer who might be left picking up the pieces due to their information being stolen. For example, their credit card is cancelled on a Friday afternoon due to the theft of information, and the customer can't use it until the new one arrives.

One thing corporations and governments need to know is that when cybercriminals break-in, one of the key steps in their checklist is to "maintain access." They'll do this by installing hidden software or rootkits that would allow them back into your systems via covert channels.

Just when you think you found the hole, you can be sure they've thought of another way through. This is why IT security audits such as penetration testing, also known as "Ethical Hacking" are important.

As Certified Ethical Hackers, we get to test the systems before the bad guys do, most of the time, anyway. When companies get hacked, consumers don't blame the cybercriminals; they blame the company.

IS THERE GOOD NEWS?

There's some good news. As a consumer, we're protected by the banks. Usually, if there are fraudulent charges on your card, you can advise your bank, and they'll be helpful.

In 2006, I wrote an article for Canada.com called "Keeping Your Identity on a Short Leash," of which most of the tips still hold true today.

Let's try an exercise shall we, go and have a look at what's in your purse or wallet and see if you're carrying any of these items which should be left at home to avoid losing them. Things like

social insurance card, passport, birth certificate, or any other cards with your social insurance number as an account number, such as a private health insurance card.

Now that our credit card and personal information is out in the wild, we can be sure to receive phone calls claiming to be from the bank or retailer, especially since the caller-id can be changed.

Here are a few tips on what cardholders should do as soon as they learn about a breach on the news.

Tip one: Banks, retailers and governments will never ask you for personal information such as your social insurance number. If they called you, you shouldn't have to provide the personal information other than a private "over the phone" password that you have arranged with the bank.

Tip two: Don't click. With all that information about you online, try not to be a Phish. Cybercriminals will be sending out mass emails to all the addresses they collected in the breach. When you receive it, they'll inform you of the breach, but then they'll ask you to click a link in order to "update your records" please don't fall for this.

Once you enter your information, it'll go straight to the bad guys who will use it against you. If you start seeing little charges on your card from one or two dollars, that means your card ended up on the black market to be sold, and the buyer is testing your card.

Tip three: Get a credit check. A credit check is an important and worthwhile investment. Consumers can order copies of their credit reports from Equifax and TransUnion Canada for about $15 to $20. These reports contain all the financial and credit history of a person, including credit cards, loans, lines of credit, as well as the phone numbers for the granting institutions. Additionally, anyone who has ever called in and requested your credit history is listed in the reports, with the date and time.

As cybercriminals become savvier, consumers must become wiser. Be alert and pay attention to how you distribute your personal information - your identity depends on it. This is also a great time to close down old credit cards you don't use anymore and help eliminate any risk to your credit.

CHAPTER FIVE

SOCIAL MEDIA SAFETY

In this chapter, I'll walk you through how to lock down your accounts on the most popular social media sites. I'll even walk you through step by step how to perform a Facebook privacy checkup, and how to spot a fake profile.

TWO-FACTOR AUTHENTICATION

Most of us understand the importance of online security, logins, usernames and passwords, but there's a good chance you've never heard of Two-factor authentication or Two-step verification. Two-factor authentication is an extra security layer that requires not only your username and password but also for a mobile phone that can receive a text message.

You'll first log into the website like normal by entering your username and password, and then, the site will send you a code directly to your mobile phone. You'll need to enter that code into the web browser, and only then can you begin using the service.

I know it sounds complicated, but you won't be prompted again on that particular device for at least 30 days. My job will be to make this as painless and straightforward as possible for you so that you get it done right.

This way, if anyone else got a hold of your password and tries to log in as you on any other device, they'll need your phone. The two factors at play are the code on your phone and your regular password.

Now, if someone figures out your password, they won't be able to get into your account unless they know the unique random code sent to your phone. You'll also know if someone is messing with your account because you'll get that text message. Two-step verification makes it harder for potential intruders to gain access and steal your data or identity. Let me show you how to enable Two-factor authentication for the most popular online services.

LINKEDIN TWO-STEP VERIFICATION

To me, LinkedIn is the most important social media account to protect. First, let's login to your account and then click your profile picture. Click on the manage link in the "PRIVACY AND SETTINGS" row.

You'll see the Two-step verification as the last item under "LOGIN AND SECURITY".

Click on "CHANGE" where we can now begin to set up the Two-step verification.

Add your phone number and choose your country and click on "SEND CODE". LinkedIn will then ask you to re-enter that code on your phone.

GOOGLE TWO-STEP VERIFICATION

Google has implemented Two-step verification across all services, which entail entering your regular password and a random number that will arrive on your mobile device.

This way, if someone does hack your password, it won't let him in without the auto-generated code in a text message that will come to your phone. Think about it? All your services are protected by one password.

GMAIL

Let's login to your account and then click your profile picture.

Once the drop-down menu appears, click on "MANAGE MY GOOGLE ACCOUNT".

Next, you'll want to click on "SECURITY" on the left menu.

Under the "SIGNING INTO GOOGLE" you have an option for Two-step verification, which is currently turned off. Let's go ahead and click.

You are in the Two-step verification wizard. Click "GET STARTED".

Next, you'll be asked the number you want to use. Enter it now and click "TRY IT".

You should have received a text message where you must enter the code that appeared on your screen. Once you've done that, click "NEXT".

You're all set. Click "TURN ON".

Hotmail

Setting Two-step verification on Hotmail is trickier.

The first thing you'll do is sign in to your Hotmail account.

Once you're in, click your picture in the top right and select "MY ACCOUNT".

Next, click on the "PROTECT YOUR ACCOUNT" icon. Next, click on the "MORE SECURITY OPTIONS" under account security.

You'll see a section called "TWO-STEP VERIFICATION".

When you go to "ENABLE" it, you'll be asked to download the "AZURE AUTHENTICATOR APP" on your mobile device.

Once you're ready to go, Hotmail will kick you out of your account. You'll need to sign back in with your username and password. You'll now be asked to enter the random code that's appearing in the Azure authenticator app.

You'll need to enter it quickly because it changes every 30 seconds.

I hope you were able to follow along and get it enabled. Just remember that all Microsoft services that you have will now require the code on the authenticator app, including Xbox Live.

FACEBOOK

Now that you're ready to secure your Facebook account, let's get started.

The first thing you're going to do is click on the little down arrow in the top right corner and then click "SETTINGS".

Click on the "SECURITY AND LOGIN" tab on the left menu pane. Once you're here, you'll have a section called "USE TWO-FACTOR AUTHENTICATION" and click "EDIT" to begin. You'll then enter your phone number, and you're all set.

ICLOUD

Open up a browser and head over to www.icloud.com. Once we're on the sign-in page, you're going to sign in using your regular Apple ID that you use to download and purchase apps. Next, click the little down arrow next to your name and choose "ACCOUNT SETTINGS".

Now that we're in the account settings page click on the "MANAGE" link. For security reasons, it's asking you to login again. What you'll see is the iCloud management page. Under the security section, there's a link to get started under the Two-step verification, go ahead and click.

Here is the hardest part.

First, you'll be prompted to answer some security questions you entered when you first created your account like 10 years ago? Apple is asking you this to make sure it's you making these changes.

Now that you've taken your trip down memory lane and successfully answered your security questions, a getting started window appears. You have to understand that once you've authorized the devices that can use iCloud, it won't prompt you again. This way, if someone guessed your password, they wouldn't be able to get into your account without the text message. Then you'll know if someone is trying to hack you.

Let's click "CONTINUE?"

Now you need to enter your mobile number that can receive text messages, then hit "CONTINUE". Check your phone, a 4-6-digit code that just arrived.

You'll need to enter those digits here. Now you'll be asked if you'd like to add any more trusted devices. If you have an iPad or have access to another iPhone, you can verify those devices here.

And we're done, congratulations.

INSTAGRAM

It's simple to activate this feature. On your mobile device, load up Instagram and click on your profile character in the bottom right corner. Once you're here, click on the "THREE BARS" icon in the top right corner.

To enable this feature, click on "SETTINGS", then on "SECURITY", and on "TWO-FACTOR AUTHENTICATION" and enter your phone number. Done.

TWITTER

Log in to your Twitter account.

Once you're in, click on "...MORE" on the left menu. Next, click on "SETTINGS AND PRIVACY".

Under the "LOGIN AND SECURITY" section, we have a "PHONE" option to verify login requests. But before we can enable this feature, we must first add our phone number by clicking on "ADD A PHONE".

Go ahead and enter your phone number now and click "CONTINUE". You should have now received a text message on your phone. You can enter those digits for Verification.

You'll have the option to be notified when you have engagement on your Twitter account. Be sure to click "SAVE CHANGES".

Now that we have our phone number registered with Twitter, you'll need to click on the "...MORE" link on the left menu tab again and click on the "SETTINGS AND PRIVACY" again. Next, we'll need to click on "ACCOUNT", "SECURITY" and then "TWO-FACTOR AUTHENTICATION".

Go ahead and click "START" to begin the final stage.

Your number should already be listed, so click on "SEND CODE" and enter the number. You can either exit or click on "GET BACKUP CODES".

It never hurts to print them and store them in a safe place.

DANGERS OF QUIZZES AND STATUS UPDATES

I want to discuss a few topics around social media quizzes and online status updates and invites. Let's start with an issue that fascinates a lot of my social media friends, but drives me nuts. I can't understand why they want to know which Disney horse resembles them or which movie star resembles them? While the quizzes are cute and all, there's a hidden agenda.

There are many quizzes set up to harvest personal information and preferences. Be wary of quizzes you have to sign into before you can start. Almost no one ever reads the fine print before they log in to a quiz app, and this is dangerous. It's dangerous because you're allowing the app to see and contact everyone on your friend's list, see your profile and copy it, and send advertising to your friends about the quiz.

Let me give you some examples. You could be doing a quiz, and the question is, "How many corners are in this image?" so you type in your answer, and next would be a question like, "What city were you born in?" Doesn't that sound a lot like a question your bank asks you when you have to verify your login?

What about status updates?

Ever read your friend's post "Woohoo - Going to Florida for a whole week. Be back next Sunday. C-ya!!! " like gee, thanks for telling the world your house is empty. I get a good laugh when I present this to fifth and sixth graders, and they respond with, "Why would anyone write that?"

Or this one "Just lost all my contacts, please text it to me at insert your number here." Now you risk getting text messages and prank calls at 4 a.m.

What about this one? "Can't wait to go to this concert tonight at the Bell Center, John Doe will be there, who else is going?" We need to keep the privacy of others in mind when you tag people without their permission.

What happens is that when you tag them and geotag them, the post shows up on their status update page, and all his friends will see where and when he'll be going. If he's called in sick to work and the boss finds out, he could get into trouble. So be courteous.

Let me tell you a quick story about social media app invites that had my friend explaining herself to her friends and coworkers. It's too funny not to share, and I wouldn't be surprised if something similar happened to you with an app. One of my long-time female friends is in a relationship for a few years now, and she got an invite from one of her contacts to join this website called Badoo.

Badoo is a site where you can meet new people and date. Anyway, not to make her contact feel bad, she decided to LIKE the app, which then asked her to sign into it using her Facebook account. She did that without reading the fine print. Moments later, her profile with all her Facebook information was automatically set up in Badoo and messages to chat with her started to flow within 10 minutes. Not only that, but her Facebook network was also notified that she joined the site.

She showed up to work the next day and coworkers began to say, "Hey, I saw that you joined Badoo, aren't you in a relationship?" or other coworkers would invite her out for a drink. Even high school friends were messaging her saying they had a crush on her 20 years ago, and they should go for coffee one night? To this day, she can't find where to close down her Badoo account.

Watch what invites you're accepting and what the app wants to do with your information.

FAKE PROFILES AND DATING SITES

Ever get added on a social media site by someone you don't know? Do you or someone you know have an account on a dating site? Maybe you're not sure if the other person behind the picture is who they are? Wouldn't you like to find out in just a few clicks instead of risking going on that date?

I know of people who've found love on sites like Plenty Of Fish or eHarmony, but they also reveal some horror stories. One of the common complaints is that their profile picture didn't look at all like him, or they wanted to meet where there weren't a lot of people.

Let me give you my top three tips to consider if you do go on that date.

Number three.

If something feels weird or off, it probably is. For example, you get invited to a house party, and the guys are getting a little crazy. You feel this could get out of hand pretty quick, and that's you're the cue to leave. I'm sure you've heard of the ole "should I bail you out phone call" where a friend calls you at a specific time, and when they do, that's when you can tell them yes, or no.

Number two.

Take friends along with you. Try to do a double date so that you can get feedback from your friends. Strength in numbers, remember that

Number one.

Always meet in a public place. Meet at a restaurant, or a bar, somewhere where cameras are watching. You'll be safer.

CHAPTER SIX

INTERNET SCAMS

With today's technology, it's almost impossible for a consumer to know they're in a scam. Internet services and websites make it easy for us to pay bills, shop, connect with anyone, make online reservations and even work, especially work from home. And you can do any of these things from anywhere in the world.

Accessibility comes at a cost. Everything you post online could one day be used in a scam against you. Banks are being robbed: now through Internet fraud. Cybercriminals have become masters at covering their tracks, creating diversions, and duping people into opting into what may seem like a great opportunity, but is actually a scam.

Today's attack methods and tools use malicious software and vulnerabilities present in programs and apps.

Being up to date on the latest patches, creating strong passwords, and being vigilant spotting fake emails is an important defence against a scam.

One significant issue I struggle with is helping to retrace phishing scammers, who have deployed attacks from unexpected regions of the world, mostly in the less developed countries.

Because of jurisdiction issues, the police can't easily reach out to catch the eventual perpetrators. Law enforcement is looking at cybercrime case-by-case, and a scam for $500 is less likely to be investigated, compared to a $5 million scam that would be investigated.

The most common way for you to become vulnerable to a malware attack or phishing scam is when you shop online, check your emails or use social media networks.

PHISHING

Phishing is the fraudulent attempt to obtain sensitive information such as usernames, passwords and credit card details by disguising oneself as a trustworthy entity in an electronic communication.

Phishing scams are based on communication made via email or on social networks. Cybercriminals will send you messages suggesting you click on a link in an attempt to steal personal information. This information could be login credentials for your bank account, social network, work account, cloud storage, your social insurance number, just to name a few.

Phishing emails will seem to come from an official source. The message could look like it came from a trusted friend asking you to click on the link, or it can be a trusted bank authority or other financial institutes, or delivery service companies, or even social network representatives.

Phishing emails look legitimate. The senders, the criminals, attempt to persuade you to click on the links to access a genuine-looking website, but are under control by the criminals. People don't pay attention to what they're clicking. Once you click, you'll receive a fake login access page that resembles the real website. Once you enter your information into the login form, the scammer will have access to your username and password in near real-time.

Scammers will create in you a sense of urgency. They'll tell you a frightening story of how your bank account is under threat and urge you to access it as soon as possible, or that there was an error in a system that you must log in to correct.

On the fake web page, you must insert your credentials to confirm your identity or your account.

In the end, after you filled in your online banking credentials, cybercriminals use that submitted information to breach your real bank account or to sell them on the dark web to other interested parties.

You can see this live "look over my shoulder" demonstration when you become a member of Internet Safety University. To learn more, please visit www.InternetSafetyUniversity.com.

THE NIGERIAN SCAM

It's known as the money laundering scam, or the 419 scams, the area code for Nigeria. This money laundering scam is one of the oldest and most popular scamming schemes. Most of us encounter in one form or another, and many have lost money. Google "Victims of Nigerian scams" to hear the heartbreaking stories.

The typical scam starts with an emotional email message. The message can come from an official government member, a businessman or a member of a very wealthy family member, usually a woman or a prince who is asking you to provide help in retrieving a large sum of money from a bank. They'll initially ask you to pay small fees for papers and legal matters. In exchange for your help, they promise you a large sum of money.

Cybercriminals will eventually ask you to pay more for additional services, such as transactions or transfer costs. You even receive papers to make you believe that it's all real. In the end, you are left broke and without any of the promised money. This scam is an expensive life lesson. The elderly are the most targeted victims of this scam, in particular, and also those who have Alzheimer's.

To add more credibility and legitimacy, these scammers are visiting genealogy sites like ancestry.com to learn more about your family heritage, hoping to discover a rich aunt or uncle. Once they find that out, they will include the information in the fake email.

GREETING CARD SCAMS

The easiest way to share your love and affection for family and friends is via an e-greeting card. Greeting card scams is an older scam but still works because scammers can make it look like it came from anyone. If you open such an email and click on the card or the links, you'll usually end up with malicious software being down-loaded and installed on your computer.

A few things could happen.

First, As we discussed in chapter three, the installed malware will launch all kinds of pop-ups with ads all over your screen. I remember the day I was working at a Hewlett Packard call centre in 1999. The morning I left for work, I received an email from my girlfriend at the time that said: "hey, check out these links."

I wasn't interested. I pressed delete. When I arrived at my desk, I had the same email in my inbox. I had a few minutes before my shift and clicked on her link.

Next thing I knew, all these pop-ups from adult sites started flooding my screen, and I couldn't close them down fast enough, so I powered off my PC. I sat back in my chair and thought, "I'm lucky."

Moments later, I hear someone in the back of the call centre saying, "Why is Terry Cutler sending me porn?"

Like I discuss in my Internet Safety Course, if your system becomes infected with such dangerous malware, you will become one of the bots, which are part of a more extensive botnet network of affected computers.

In this unfortunate event, your computer will start sending private data, and financial information to a fraudulent server or your PC will attack other companies because criminals are now in control.

BANK LOAN OR CREDIT CARD SCAM

People going through difficult financial times could get trapped by "too good to be true" bank offers. These offers claim to guarantee you significant amounts of money and have already been pre-approved by the bank.

No interest credit cards are appealing. If you receive such an incredible pre-approved loan, use common sense to judge if it's real.

Think about it? How on earth is it possible for a bank to contact you and offer you such a large sum of money without even knowing your financial situation?

You would think, "who'd fall for that?" There's still a significant number of people who lost money by paying the "mandatory" processing fees required by the scammers.

LOTTERY SCAM

The fraud begins as an email message informing you that you won a considerable amount of money, and all you need to do to collect your fortune is to pay some small fees. Just the thought of quitting our jobs and going to live on a beach somewhere while living off the fortunes for the rest of our lives would make us interested.

I mean, the idea alone can make our imaginations fall prey to images of an oceanfront dream house, endless summer vacations or expensive items. In the real world, the dream ends as soon as you realize you've been another sucker in a scam.

ROMANCE SCAMS

Have you or anyone you know been fooled by a romance scam? You've seen the emails. "I'm Yuliana, and I'm from Ukraine and want to get to know you better. Here's my picture."

This scam takes place on social networks such as dating sites, Facebook, or by receiving a simple email.

To gain your trust, this con job may take place for several months. In many cases, it can even get to a point with an in-person meeting. At this point, two things may take place.

An "unpredictable" event occurs, and the scammer needs money as soon as possible for his/her passport or other details. Or worse, if you come from a wealthy family, you may be "fake" kidnapped, and a large sum of money could be the demand for your safe return.

you receive a suspicious call, hang up. If you have concerns about your taxes, contact the CRA.

COMPUTER VIRUS TELEMARKETING SCAM

Have you received a call from "John Smith" with the thick Indian accent pretending to represent Microsoft or Apple, informing you that your computer has a virus? To "fix" the problem, you'll be asked to go to a website, where they'll ask you to install remote control software for them to log in to your computer. Once you've allowed them in, they'll download a fake antivirus that will lock your PC and force you to provide your credit information to make a payment to unlock your PC.

For the record, companies like Apple and Microsoft will never contact you if there's a problem with your computer. You're responsible for keeping your software up to date.

Always be skeptical and vigilant when you receive these types of calls. Ask for a call back number, or Google their phone number while you have them on the phone to see if anyone reported it as a scam. Remember never to give your personal or banking information to anyone unless you are confident you can trust the source. Remember to report the fraud to law enforcement to keep them informed.

SMISHING (SMS PHISHING)

Short Message Service (SMS) is the technology used for text messages on cell phones. SMS phishing uses cell phone text messages to deliver the bait to induce people to divulge their personal information. Smishing means SMS Phishing. You'll receive Bogus text messages in an attempt to lure you into unknowingly agreeing to accept hefty monthly charges to your credit card.

They then download a virus, or malware onto your smartphone or other mobile devices.

Smishing texts often use "trending" news and entertainment topics or use aggressive threats of fake-billings to lure you to a fraudulent website. That's where you'll get asked to enter sensitive information such as credit card details or passwords. When you receive these texts, delete them and don't click the link.

ONLINE SECOND-HAND SHOPPING

Are you using sites like eBay, Amazon, Facebook GarageSale or Kijiji?

It may not have happened to you, but consumers that use online second-hand shopping and social media sites have found themselves getting ripped off or giving out private information to a stranger. Rip-offs usually include misrepresentation of the product, purchasing a fake or broken product, paying too much or paying upfront and never receiving the item. Other dangerous situations include giving out private information about home or family to an unknown stranger, risking identity theft and robbery.

When shopping online, use extreme caution and make sure you truly understand who you are doing business with and the risk associated with doing business with strangers. Ask detailed questions about the product or service you want to purchase. Ask for the product serial number and do your research to ensure you understand what fair market value is and to see if anyone reported it stolen. If you need to meet to make an in-person trade, be sure to do so in a public location or make the visit with a trusted friend. If it sounds too good to be true?

COUNTERFEIT MERCHANDISE

The Internet is ideal for the proliferation of online stores and auction sites marketing alluring, cheaply priced, counterfeit products pitched as the real thing.

Legitimate Gucci handbags and Rolex watches don't come cheap, no matter what the sale price. Before you buy any product online, do your research to help you spot the differences between a real and a fake item.

PRESIDENCY SCAM OR THE CEO/CFO SCAM

This scam usually happens in a business setting.

The Chief Financial Officer will receive an email that looks like it came from the CEO asking the Chief Financial Officer, or CFO, to secretly wire transfer funds to another bank account. Presidency scams are highly sophisticated scams based on dedicated research before any contact with the target. The scammers will recon you, so if you're in a situation where you acquired another company, for example, the scammers will find out and tailor the message about funds needed for a particular project relating to the merger. A lot of companies have fallen for this.

In one of my investigations, cybercriminals hacked into a non-profit organization's email system and began monitoring and reading employee emails for at least six months. The organization was ready to receive new funding for a new project when the cybercriminals intercepted the email chain and asked for the funds to be transferred to another bank account.

Because the cybercriminals had access to their documents with bank information and a scanned signature of the president, the funder transferred $480,000 USD in funding to an offshore account as instructed.

THE GRANDPARENT SCAM

The Grandparent Scam is nerve-wracking. Senior citizens receive a frantic phone call from what appears to be their grandson or granddaughter, nephew or niece, saying, while crying about how they've been arrested and need money for bail.

The phone is handed off to another person who claims to be the arresting officer. He asks for the elderly's credit card for the bail money, and if they don't have one, they'll send a courier over to pick up the money.

When the grandparent finally speaks with the grandson or nephew, the youngster has no idea what the grandparent was talking about and that he's okay.

CHAPTER SEVEN

MOBILE SECURITY

At home we can plug into one or more devices such as computers, printers, game consoles, your fridge and toaster, and whatever else has a network jack.

"The Internet of Things," which is a term used for new smart devices and connected homes accessible from anywhere in the world is here, and that opens an entirely new can of worms when it comes to security. Cybercriminals have already started breaking into refrigerators and using their connection to attack other networks.

THE ROUTER

A router, in most cases, has four colourful identical ports and one different port. The different one is the plug-in for your Internet modem, which will allow the other devices in your home to surf the Internet. The four same colour ports are where you can insert your PC or printer. Once you're all plugged up and ready to go, the network should be automatically set up as well as the Internet.

When installing your router, the default login information is typical: Username admin, password, admin. It's paramount that we change this to a different and stronger password. Hopefully, you read the chapter on how to create strong passwords. If you don't change this password, a hacker can log in and discover the devices in your network. Or a neighbour might decide to connect to your Wi-Fi and use up your bandwidth instead of paying for an Internet bill.

Bandwidth hijacking is common in university dorm settings.

In 2011, a Concordia University student in Montreal, Canada, was hit with a few hundred dollars overcharge for exceeding her download limit because other students were connected to her Wi-

Fi network and downloading pirated music and movies. That's why I chuckle when I hear people say, "I don't care. I don't have anything important on my network." Let's make sure this doesn't happen to you.

Keep in mind, it's difficult stopping a determined cybercriminal, so the goal is to make it as hard as possible. Since I'm trained to think and act like a hacker on behalf of the good guys, let's implement a few protective settings.

Every router interface will be slightly different, but the functions are similar. Once you've logged in, you'll want to go to your administration section and change your password. At least 16-25 characters are suitable for a password, as we discussed earlier.

You can begin by clicking on the wireless tab.

You'll notice a section called BAND. BAND will allow you to set up a 2.4ghz and a 5ghz network. If we click the pull-down, you can see two options. The primary differences between the 2.4GHz and 5GHz wireless frequencies are range and bandwidth. 5GHz provides faster data rates at a shorter distance, whereas 2.4GHz offers coverage for farther distances, but may perform at slower speeds.

I like to label the 2.4GHz channel with different network names since my old devices like the iPad generation one can connect. All the newer devices use the 5ghz channel, and it's faster.

There's a couple of things to check on this page. If we look at the "HIDE SSID" feature, this will hide your network from broadcasting. It means that you have to know the exact name of the Wi-Fi network, its password and other settings to connect.

Some believe that if you hide the SSID that it won't be found. There are ways to find out how many wireless devices are connected. What I care most about is the Authentication method. For home users, you want to use WPA2-Personal with the encryption level of AES.

Next, we need to create a strong password known as a "WPA-PRE-SHARED KEY" that will be used to connect to the Wi-Fi network. WPA stands for Wi-Fi Protected Access. Please don't use the same password as the Administrator code. You'll want to create a 16-25-character password using a combination of upper case, lower case symbols and numbers. Let's do that for both the 2.4Ghz channel and 5Ghz.

If we click on the "WIRELESS MAC FILTERING" tab, you'll have a chance to enable this security feature. Every Internet-connected device will have a different unique MAC address. A MAC address is a unique number associated with the network card in your PC or phone, and no two MAC addresses are the same.

When this feature is enabled, only the device you type in or select from the dropdown can connect to your network. Anything else will not be allowed to authenticate unless you add the address to the network.

Adding an address is difficult to manage because every time you have visitors who want to connect to your Wi-Fi, you'll need to add their device first before they can use your network. Security is not about convenience.

To find a MAC address on an iPhone, go into the "SETTINGS" app, "GENERAL" then "ABOUT". Now scroll to the bottom and look for the Wi-Fi address. That's the number you'll add to your list to allow your visitors access.

To locate the MAC address of your Android phone or tablet, click on the Home screen, tap the Menu key and go to "SETTINGS" Scroll down and tap "ABOUT TABLET" then tap "STATUS" and then scroll down to "VIEW WI-FI MAC ADDRESS."

MONITORING YOUR TRAFFIC

Under the "TRAFFIC MANAGER" tab, click on "TRAFFIC MONITORING". This feature allows you to see if there's a substantial traffic load on your network. Traffic Monitoring is helpful for people that haven't secured their router.

They'd be sitting there wondering why their modem lights are blinking, and their Internet is slow.

PARENTAL CONTROLS

There are studies showing that kids are going to school exhausted in the morning because they are online through all hours of the early morning. Remember, if your child is using an iPhone or an Android, they can disconnect from your Wi-Fi and your parental controls and use the 5g data service, which will provide them unrestricted access. The best option is to take the device and return it to them in the morning.

WHAT YOU DON'T KNOW ABOUT PUBLIC WI-FI

At times, we may want free Wi-Fi to help preserve our precious data plan. The problem is, you're just searching and connecting to the first hotspot that doesn't have a lock next to it, symbolizing it's free.

As a professional ethical hacker, I'm not only going to show you how to gain access to usernames and passwords; I'm going to teach you the insider secrets of Wi-Fi safety.

Millions of passwords are stolen each day. Cybercriminals typically hangout at hotels, cafés, restaurants and other public areas and have their computer loaded up and configured as a Wi-Fi hotspot. This way, when you show up for your $10 Latte, you can conveniently surf the web.

Watch out for Wi-Fis with the same name except it says free somewhere. As an example, when I stayed at a Marriott hotel, I tried to connect to Wi-Fi. The hotel required a password or last name and room number combination. I saw "Marriott hotel Free public Wi-Fi," but it went offline shortly after I connected. I'm not sure why. Here's why.

Cybersecurity experts and cybercriminals use software known as sniffers. Sniffer software allows anyone to eavesdrop, intercept and even record a phone conversation via your Internet. For example, communications going back and forth between your social media accounts, sensitive corporate data, and where your surfing is available through a sniffer.

If I were trying to sniff you while you were connected to the same public Wi-Fi as me or one used by a cybercriminal, most of your data would be normally encrypted or scrambled. However, if you're connected to a fake Wi-Fi, a sniffer allows the interception of your data as it is being transmitted.

Sniffing is known as a "Man-in-the-middle" attack.

Not only can anyone snoop on your communication, but also have the capability to redirect you to legitimate-looking sites that may infect your computer, where we keyloggers can be installed in your computer. Keyloggers record everything you are typing on your keyboard into a file to be retrieved later. This way, if you're logging into bank accounts, typing your social insurance number into government websites, or typing emails, every character you type can be used to steal your identity.

Smartphones are particularly vulnerable to such attacks since most people have enabled the automatic connection option, which will connect the device to any Wi-Fi network. The device may connect to such fake Wi-Fi networks, and steal your username and password for your email accounts if they aren't set up with secure email settings.

The critical thing to look for while surfing online and entering login information is the lock icon on the browser's address bar. This ensures the communication stream is safe and encrypted.

If a security message shows up on your smartphone informing you that your email is trying to communicate with a system like Google mail, or that the server's security certificate doesn't match the system, someone is attempting to intercept you.

It's time to disconnect from that FREE public Wi-Fi and use your hotspot on your cell phone. If you're using your laptop in an open area, you can enable a "PERSONAL HOTSPOT" on your phone and use that Wi-Fi communication instead of the hostile FREE one.

If you take your iPhone and go to your settings app and choose "PERSONAL HOTSPOT" you have the option to enable it. Once it's on, it'll show up on the Wi-Fi list. Click to connect and type in the password listed on your phone.

You now have your little secure hotspot.

CHAPTER EIGHT

ACRONYMS AND ABBREVIATIONS

During Internet Safety talks with parents when I mention basic chat words like BRB, LOL, IMHO, OMG, they look at me as if I was a mumbling fool.

According to a survey done by SurveilStar - Kids Internet Safety, 95 percent of parents did not recognize chat room lingo used by their children/teens to let people they're talking to know that parents were watching. More than 64 percent of teens say they do things online they would never want their parents to know about.

This chapter will take you to Internet school.

We will learn about the Internet lingo kids are using every day. I need to warn you that I will be covering adult content, foul language and porn slangs, so you can use this new-found knowledge to decode some of the terms you're finding in your mobile or computer's search history.

It's important that you know these acronyms if you have young children.

Let's start with the basics.

BRB – Be right back

Lol – laugh out loud

Lmao – laugh my ass off

YOLO – You only live one

2moro – Tomorrow

BTW - By The Way

B4N - Bye For Now

BFF - Best Friends Forever

CYA – could mean Cover Your Ass or just… See Ya

DBEYR - Don't Believe Everything You Read

DILLIGAS - Do I Look Like I Give A Shit

FWIW - For What It's Worth
GR8 – Great
ILY - I Love You
IMHO - In My Humble Opinion
IRL - In Real Life
ISO - In Search Of
J/K - Just Kidding
L8R - Later
NP - No Problem -or- Nosy Parents
NUB - New person to a site or game, basically a beginner
OIC - Oh, I See
ROTFLMAO - Rolling On The Floor Laughing My Ass Off
TFH - Thread From Hell
TMI - Too Much Information
TTYL - Talk To You Later
WTF - What The F***
WYWH - Wish You Were Here
XOXO - Hugs and Kisses

These Acronyms and Abbreviations are used with most texting conversions. Have you ever heard of Emojis? If not, then for sure, you've seen them.

They are cute little smiley faces, and thumbs up, and angry faces, sad faces, but what happens when you go on your kid's phone and see this?

Now let me take you to the darker side of texting and sexting called Net-speak. These acronyms are used to keep parents clueless and what every parent needs to look out for. If you see this in your child's conversations with a friend, these are red flags and need to be reported.

ASL - Age, Sex, Location... This is one of the first questions a predator will ask.
ASLP - Age, Sex, Location, Picture
TDTM - Talk Dirty To Me
GNOC - Get Naked On Cam

$46 - This means Money For Sex
LMIRL - Let's Meet In Real Life.
IPN - I'm Posting Naked
WTTP - Want To Trade Photos
CU46 - See You For Sex
53X - Sex
SUGARPIC - A Suggestive or Erotic Photo
PRON - Porn
20.8 - Oral Sex
LH6 - Let's Have Sex
ADR - Address
GYPO - Get Your Pants Off
IWSN - I Want Sex Now
KFY - Kiss For You
KPC - Keeping Parents Clueless
P911 - Parent Alert
99 – Parents are gone
PAL - Parents Are Listening
PAW - Parents Are Watching
PIR - Parent In Room
p0rn/porn — Both short for pornography, often misspelled on purpose in texts to avoid detection.
POS - Parent Over Shoulder
WYCM - Will You Call Me
WGTP - Want To Go Private
F2F - Face To Face.

"Sexting" has become mainstream in society. You can even download a sexting emoji keyboard from the Apple or Google's App Store called Lifestyles.

Now that I've shocked you with that last emoji, let's explore other ones being used

This means Genitalia.

These are the emojis to describe a guy's private parts.

These are the emojis to describe a girl's private parts.

These are the emojis to describe a girl's breasts.

These are the emojis to describe intercourse.

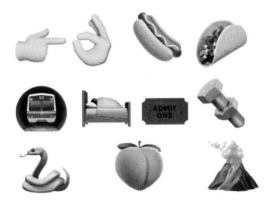

These are the emojis to describe "Manual stimulation"

Wow, I think we've covered enough. This concludes this tutorial on Acronyms and abbreviations. There's no doubt you learnt something new, so be sure to pass on your new-found knowledge to others.

CHAPTER NINE

TIGHTENING YOUR COMPUTER SECURITY

Most of the computers I am asked to inspect are already infected. The problem, in many cases, is enabled access facilitates a virus infection.

In this chapter, first, I'll walk you through how to correct this on a MAC and PC. We'll perform a checkup to ensure your browser's configuration is ready for safe and convenient browsing.

Second, I'll guide you by using simple tools that allow you to find out if you've already been hacked or being spied on by cyber-criminals, or by someone you know.

ENABLING AUTOMATIC UPDATES ON WINDOWS

Have you ever been in a situation where you're shutting down your computer to rush to a meeting and Windows decides to tell you it's now installing 134 new updates? Automatic updates occur every Tuesday.

We call it Patch Tuesday.

It's essential to keep current with Windows updates, especially security updates. These updates contain so many new operating system bug fixes and for others such as virus definitions for Windows Defender, Microsoft Office and Internet Explorer.

Keeping up to date with these security fixes is the first step in defending yourself while online.

New viruses and scams are continually trying to find ways into your PC, so we must stay up to date. Let's go ahead now and make sure your computer is set to automatically download and install updates.

INSTALLING AND MAINTAINING ANTIVIRUS SOFTWARE

Every computer needs to have antivirus software installed. It's that software that slows your computer down to a grind, but it's a necessary evil.

Antivirus software is designed to continually scan for threats such as attachments in your incoming mail, scanning files that you download, open, and access. Some antivirus software even comes with intrusion prevention capabilities.

It's also important to know that just because you have an antivirus installed, it doesn't mean you're safe. Antivirus technology is signature-based. Every time you update, it downloads a database of known viruses. This way, when it scans your PC, it can say, "I know this type of virus, so I'm going to block it."

A question asked often is, what's the difference between a free antivirus and a paid version, and which one is the best? Most antivirus vendors use a concept called freemium. It means that potentially millions of people download and use the free version in exchange for feedback. Even though it's free, there are some hidden costs.

Free versions don't come with the advanced scanning capability as the paid versions. All you need is one undetected virus to get through, and you'll spend more time and money on cleaning up your PC, calling online identity protection services and closing down credit cards.

The paid version vendors collect feedback and virus incidents from its global user community and compile that information into a paid version. The paid version now has so many features beyond the knowledge of a free antivirus version.

For example, when you upgrade to a paid version, you typically get advanced firewall features that not only block threats to your computer, but it can also stop malicious communication from leaving your computer. You typically get email scanning security. Each time you receive an email, the virus scanner will scan your attachments to make sure you're safe.

Paid versions also come with a communications protector. For example, say you use Skype or Facebook messenger, when someone sends you a file, the antivirus will scan that in real-time.

These are just a few features that a paid antivirus version has over the free ones. With the new advances in cyber-attacks, it's worth upgrading to the paid version.

Which one is the best? According to TomGuide.com, Avira antivirus got the editor's choice with a 9/10 score.

I'll discuss MAC at the end of this section, but for now, Windows 7, 8 and 10 come with a free built-in virus protection system called Windows Defender. If you're using an older version of Windows, know that you're unsupported by Microsoft, and no updates are available.

There is another well-known antivirus software out there such as Symantec, Kaspersky and McAfee. If you run a small or medium-sized business, you can check out hosted antivirus solutions like Symantec EndPoint protection, where you can see and manage all computers in one place.

Only install one antivirus application unless you want your computer to be slow from continually scanning your system in double. Sometimes you might be unaware that you've established a second antivirus because you went and installed some free software, which introduced a Yahoo toolbar and installed a free antivirus at the same time. That usually happens to folks who don't read the prompts and click next, next, next all the way through.

You should become familiar with more specialized malware and spyware prevention software. One of my favourites is Malwarebytes anti-malware. You can download that from malwarebytes.org. I've had success and highly recommend the Paid Pro version.

You can download it for both Mac and Windows. It's worth purchasing for the extra protection.

The other app is called CCLEANER from piriform.com. This tool will scan your system's registry, clean out unwanted temporary files and optimize your PC.

It can also let you look at what programs are starting up with Windows in case you've been installing the software you shouldn't have, and your computer is running slow.

When I am hired to hack into companies, I often go around to unattended computers and plug in my USB drive to steal usernames, passwords and sometimes sensitive files. These above options should detect my programs, but they're not because they aren't enabled.

MAC

I get into debates about whether or not Macs get viruses. Do Macs need antivirus software? The short answers are yes, and yes. As I discussed in the "Installing updates on your Mac" Internet Safety University tutorial, viruses usually get on a MAC because we accidentally installed it, but you need to know that it's much more challenging to get a virus on a MAC than a PC.

Let me walk you through a malware removal tool that has saved my clients and me tons of headaches called Malwarebytes anti-malware for MAC and PC.

First, open up your browser and go towww.Malwarebytes.org. Once you're on the home screen, click on the "FOR HOME" at the top. Next, you'll want to click on the "MAC" tab at the bottom.

Then click "DOWNLOAD" in the middle.

The next question is, "If you want the Home edition or the Business edition?" What we want to click on is below that which says "TO PROTECT YOUR MAC, GO HERE". Now we're on the Mac download page, so click "DOWNLOAD". The file is now in your download folder, so let's find it and install it. Next, we'll drag the malware bytes into our applications folder to begin the installation.

Now that it's installed, scroll down in the Applications folder to Malwarebytes and double click to launch. You're getting prompted for a warning that this is an application downloaded from the Internet.

An unsafe application is an example of how a virus can find its way to a MAC. Because Apple never digitally signed this application as safe, it's up to the user to make a sound judgement. Since we trust this application, let's click "OPEN" and then "ACCEPT" the license agreement.

Now you're being prompted to enter the system password to make sure you do want to run this software. Go ahead and enter your password. Now you have three options. Click the scan button. If it found anything on your MAC, you'd be prompted on whether or not you want to fix the issue.

PHYSICALLY PROTECT YOUR COMPUTER FROM THREATS

I want to talk to you about physically safeguarding your computer from threats. If a malicious person has physical access to your computer, your data could be stolen easily using simple hacker tools.

I won't cover how to hack into other people's computers. But I can tell you that if I had physical access to your computer, I could reboot it and insert my USB stick, which would allow me to change your password or even blank it out so that there is no password, without even knowing your password.

Let's discuss some other ways to make it difficult for your computer to be compromised and avoid business interruption.

First, the most important thing to take away is to back up your data. When we talked about ransomware scams earlier, you learned why. If you get hit with ransomware, all your data gets encrypted and is completely unusable until you pay a ransom to the bad guys to get a key to unlock your stuff. So far, there's no way to decrypt this data. Even the FBI tells companies and individuals to pay the ransom.

Windows has a built-in backup software, or you can look at other solutions like Cloud backup. Other tools are called Carbonite and Veeam, which will update your data based on custom settings as frequently as you require.

Second, learn to lock your computer when you leave your desk. Back in the day, we used to prank people that didn't lock their computers by emailing the team, saying they're paying for lunch. Today, the consequences of leaving your computer unlocked are much more severe. I carry a USB key full of security tools that if I plugged it into an unlocked computer, I could extract every username and password on it in 14 seconds. That's why you should never let a stranger use your computer.

It's essential to lock your screen when you walk away. To lock a Windows system, hold down the Windows key and hit L on your keyboard. This action is going to lock your screen instantly.

If you're using a Mac, hold down the control key and the shift key together and press the eject key.

Third, what about passwords and Post-it notes? I often see on desks or bulletin boards, stuck to their monitors or under the keyboard, where there's a sticker of the username and password for their PC.

If you see someone like that, do tell them about this book?

Fourth, buy a cable lock. If you're not sure what this is, it's a lock that clips into your computer and can wrap around furniture, making it harder for someone to walk off with it, especially if you're in a hotel room.

Here's a quick tip, hang the "Do Not Disturb" sign when you leave the room. You never know what hotel employee would be tempted to get into your room and steal your stuff. This way, they'll think someone is still in the place.

And fifth, try to avoid using public Wi-Fi. They're unsafe. Please turn on the hotspot on your mobile phone and surf off that connection where you know it's safe.

CHANGING FROM AN ADMIN USER TO STANDARD USER

You've probably heard MAC users laughing hysterically in the face of PC users when it comes to viruses and hacks, and there are a few reasons why.

The reason is that when Windows is installed for the first time, it's creating an administrator user account that you'll use by default, which has unrestricted access on your computer and can also modify anyone else's account on the same PC.

Sounds fantastic right, and it can be, that is, until something goes wrong like a virus or hack. Viruses will run with the same permissions as your current logged in user. If it's the administrator account, the virus can infect your entire computer.

MAC has the reverse. Their user account has limited functionality to customize their computer, and because of this, it also protects critical system files that keep the computer's operating system functioning.

The other reason is that there are fewer viruses created for MAC. For a virus to end up on the MAC, the user would have to allow it by entering the administrator password for it to install.

For this reason, Windows is a much higher-value target. It's far less work for a lazy spammer or cybercriminal to get a virus installed on Windows simply because the PC is already set up with all the access it needs to run with little help from the user.

The good news is we can change that so that you can have similar security as the MAC folks.

The first thing we're going to do is open the "ADVANCED USER CONTROL PANEL". Now the beauty is that this utility works on Windows 7, 8 and 10, and it looks very similar so it won't be confusing. I'm going to use Windows 10 to launch this utility, push the "START" button, and then type NETPLWIZ and press enter.

This utility will show you all the users you have added on your computer. The chances are that your user is part of the administrator's group, which is what we want to re-configure. If you only have one user setup like I do in this demonstration, then you must pay attention to these next steps, or you will not be able to manage your computer again without using hacking tools to regain control of your account.

Before we remove the administrator-level access from your user account, we need to first create and replace it with a new user with administrator access controls. Now that we're in the User account wizard, let's click the "ADD" button to create a new user.

Next, you will see the question of "HOW WILL THIS PERSON SIGN IN". This question is new to Windows 8 and 10 because they're allowing you to sign in with your Hotmail account. This way, all your documents, pictures, browser history and more can all be synchronized to your other Windows devices.

Create a new user by using the new method and then I'll demonstrate the Windows 7 alternative way, which also works on Windows 8 and 10.

I'll enter my Hotmail email address and let Windows do its magic. You'll notice that it's advising you to connect to the Internet to login. Let's click "FINISH".

You'll notice we created a new user with your email address, but it only has standard user privileges. If you double click on the new user, we can now make changes. Feel free to enter the general information, but we care about the "GROUP MEMBERSHIP" tab where we can upgrade this user from a standard user to an administrator. Go ahead and click "ADMINISTRATOR" then click "APPLY" and "OK".

Now that we have two administrator users, we can double click the default user that you always use to log in, and we'll downgrade it to a standard user. We'll do this by again going to the "GROUP MEMBERSHIP" tab, and this time we'll choose standard users, then click "APPLY" and "OK".

You should see a pop-up that says, "You've made changes to this user account and must sign out and in again for the changes to take effect". Click "YES" to sign out.

Notice that you have another user to choose from on the left-hand side? We'll keep using our regular user, and whenever you want to install new software, it will prompt you to type in the administrator password.

Go ahead and sign in with your regular user, and I'll show you an example of what would happen now. I'll finish signing in myself, and I want to open up Microsoft Edge, formally Internet Explorer. I'll go to a random website like Itunes.com.

The iTunes app is like a central entertainment hub for your music, shows and movies. I'll click on "DOWNLOAD" in the top right, and now I'll choose my language of choice, and then click "DOWNLOAD NOW".

The download will take about five minutes. Once the download is complete, click "RUN". iTunes will initialize the install files, and you'll see a welcome to iTunes screen.

Select "NEXT" and then choose "INSTALL".

Now you're faced with typing in the administrator password to install this application or any application. There are some cases where you won't be asked for the administrator password because the application can be installed just for you and not affect anything else on the computer.

An example of this is Google Chrome.

Open Edge again and go to google.com/chrome. Once you're on the page, select "DOWNLOAD NOW".

Leave the defaults and click "ACCEPT AND INSTALL".

Notice that you still get prompted, but if you hit cancel, you get a message that you can install Google Chrome without administrator privileges, and do you want to continue? Choose "YES" and let the install finish.

As you can see, not all applications need to have administrator level access to install, which is great because that means you can contain an infected app.

However, if you're installing an application that you've obtained illegally from the web and I know you'd never do that, and you tried to install it, and it prompts you for the administrator password, and you enter it, guess what? You've just permitted the virus to infect the entire PC.

Remember, the weakest link in all of cybersecurity is us, humans.

To learn about any new steps to any of these above-discussed processes, visit www.InternetSafetyUniversity.com

PART TWO

CHAPTER TEN

YOU'RE THE CSO

Your cell phone rings at 3 a.m. Before you pick up, you know what's happening. As the company's network Chief Security Officer (CSO), you've known this was a possibility. A cybercriminal has hacked your network.

The assistant security specialist in your global company is sorry to wake you, but it couldn't wait. He has spotted what he's calling "highly" suspicious activity over the company network. He has no idea "what" is happening, and although he's monitoring the problem, the situation is expected to worsen.

You dress in jeans and a T-shirt and begin the long drive to the office. In the meantime, customer service representatives are reporting numerous complaints of unauthorized debits to their credit cards and banks, your customer service department is dealing with irate customer calls, and the backlog is mounting. No one is happy. What do we tell our customers? The media? Didn't someone in IT last week say the network was slower than usual? Last month you did find a new user account with an unknown origin.

Could that be it?

What about those unauthorized usage times? Unexplained addition, deletion, or modification of data did raise some suspicion last year, but you cleaned that, right? The tech department one month ago recommended a complete shutdown, a stopgap measure, in the event of an attack. You considered the possibility.

Your secretary is now on your smartphone and informs you three credit card companies are on hold, wanting answers, and the CEO of one of your top customers has called three times. You look at your smartphone and wonder who is listening. How many smartphones did we issue to our employees?

Your mind is still churning. Was all that training on Internet security worth it? Could it be as simple as a silly email, a phish?

"Hi, this is a computer company XYZ and your CEO authorized me to get the model number on the modem?"

That's too easy, you tell yourself. The employees are up to date on these social engineering scams. Aren't they? Who from outside could have done this?

What about that flower delivery man last week? He came rather early, didn't he? How long did he linger around the office? The sanitation worker? What about the night security guard you fired a month ago? You think about that memo you received from IT security to advise all employees not to write passwords of sensitive information on those yellow Post-its.

Did you fire any IT personnel lately? Did any IT employee suddenly resign? Back to the Post-it notes? Could it have been as easy as a password scribbled on a Post-it notes pinned to a bulletin board?

You've known all along, and on your way to work (the longest drive of your life) and you admit it: someone may be inside your network.

How's this possible?

You've provided the training. You made sure your employees were checked and double-checked. You have gone from posting a sign at the entrance stating, "Loose lips sink ships" to "Internet Network Security Awareness is Everybody's Business." Your employee security training is up to date, you remind yourself, or try to convince yourself, and you've hired the best security people you could find. More doubt sets in.

Last week you sent out a memo reminding your employees surfing bulletin boards or Facebook at work is against security policy. Did an employee click on an attractive link? You've thought of this day.

It's here.

The truth is, you didn't work to prevent an attack but rather to make an attack difficult. Don't feel your company is the only one being attacked and don't take it personally. You have prepared for this eventuality. Check your ego at the door.

Cybercriminals have all day to find ways to get into your network. Once in, they can lurk around in your network, looking for the tiniest of loopholes in the codes. You're not surprised you got a phone call at 3 a.m.

You might take some joy if your team detected the breach, and because of your diligence, you're feeling confident that you will prevent any further penetration.

Your confidence should be at an all-time high. You remind yourself, employees, support staff and executives in the company know how to spot or become suspicious about possible threats that could unleash a virus on a computer by simply opening an email with a malicious program. Your forward-thinking is making it easier to find through which port. You're ready.

NEVER DELETE THE EVIDENCE

Your proactive approach shouldn't become reactive. Now is the time to kick it into high gear. The realization someone has hacked into the network triggers an immediate response to shut it all down. The feeling is "pull the plug and cut access to the attacker," and by doing that, the attack stops, you hope.

It makes sense, at first, but it can make future investigation difficult. Evidence will be wiped clean.

You may never know who the cybercriminal is, or what data was stolen, if any? Shutting down the network may be a knee-jerk reaction to a problem easily solved, but you will never know - you threw the switch.

The same applies to a sophisticated cybercriminal who has spent months lurking under the surface, wielding fake emails in spear-phishing attempts, decoding your barriers and gaining access to small bits of sensitive information. Do. Not. Wipe. Your.

Computers. The hacker may even be counting on you shutting down. Your legal team will want a forensic report.

Gather information from all departments, and don't be afraid to examine all the possibilities.

While much of the focus was on teaching security to employees, someone higher up the ladder might have unknowingly done something to allow access to the attacker. It could be as simple as an executive using a laptop in an open coffee shop, or a Starbucks hack. Keep asking questions. How significant is the problem? Is it one computer, or the entire network, or somewhere in between? Has IT noted any peculiar employee behaviour? Are any logs suggesting suspicious practices?

GET HELP FROM AN INCIDENT RESPONSE SPECIALIST

Once you're at the office, you set your plan in motion. The damage assessment is underway. Customer service is aware of the problem, and you've instructed the customer service supervisor on how to speak with your customers.

You may be able to handle the incident alone, but as a top CSO, you've learned more heads result in positive outcomes. You might call in a cybersecurity expert. Cybersecurity experts are people who can help you prevent an attack and determine its origin, and are experts at breaking into your system just like a cybercriminal.

Cybersecurity experts are known as "white hats," doing the same work as cybercriminals known as "black hats," but for ethical reasons. Ethical hackers are up to date on the latest cutting-edge technology and the most recent breaches 24 hours a day. Usually, a company has worked with an ethical hacker. As CSO, you more than once watched over an ethical hacker's shoulder as he or she penetrated your system right before your eyes. You've seen the "hacking" possibilities.

Customers will blame you for any personal losses. Let's say credit card numbers are being lifted off the company database.

Nothing reaps havoc on the mind like knowing if your credit card number is "out there" somewhere and in the hands of shady characters. Breached companies will usually post a notification letter on their website, explaining the situation and assuring customers they are working on the problem, and everything is under control.

As CSO, you're aware of the value of reassuring customers and keeping them as valued customers. A company's reputation, if founded on quality customer service, will help soften the blow that may come to the company's established reputation.

To Report or Not to Report?

The tendency to disconnect is followed by the desire to remain quiet about being hacked.

What's becoming clear is more companies are reporting their attacks, leading to more useful data sharing among companies. In a sense, detailing all breaches to legal Internet Security forces is a way to stockpile and analyze types of hacks, methods used, and what to be on the lookout for to make it more difficult.

As the CSO, you begin to reconsider ongoing penetration and social engineering testing. But, you either don't have a budget for a real assessment, or you are satisfied with a "pass" on the way to compliance, which doesn't mean you are secure.

In fairness, we cannot expect companies or products to catch all potential intrusions.

Your next phone call: the news that your team has prevented the penetration. The report is music to your ears. Now, you begin to work on preventing the next penetration attempt.

Continued cybersecurity testing is key. You call in an ethical hacker.

HOW I WOULD HACK YOUR NETWORK

As a cybercriminal, I know companies don't take cybersecurity as seriously as they should. IT is often allocated the smallest portion of the overall budget, and managers don't see the need for security until it's too late.

Here's how I would hack your company if I turned to the dark side.

Step 1 – Recon: It wouldn't take me long to find your employees on social media. I would find out their interests, their connection, and the best email to reach them. I may even find out where the CEO lives, drive to his house and scan his unsecured WIFI. I may even leave a few USB sticks around your office, or leave a USB key in the urinal?

There's so much information I can find out about your organization from various sources, and I haven't even touched your organization yet. The job postings some companies put out there are revealing way too much information about what software is running inside the company. Guess what? There's nothing you can do about it because it's required to do business.

Step 2 – Scanning: I've spent a day or so mounting my battle plan, and now I'm going to scan your network to find out what systems are online, what software you're running, and how many vulnerabilities exist for each of your software. We "hackers" have an effective support system where we share information about how to breach a certain technology.

Step 3 – Attack: Now that my VPN is set up, and I've now changed my IP address to leave the impression I'm operating in another country, just to mess with your IT department.

Here's the thing, I don't have time to waste trying to crack your firewall and risk being detected, when all I have to do is send a compelling email with a link to your employee I befriended a few days ago.

Your employee won't think it's a scam, so they'll click on my link and let me right into the network almost undetected. I say almost because the incident may have been logged in somewhere in your systems, but the IT department isn't trained in detection.

For the record, your firewall and antivirus won't save you. We "hackers" have access to specialized training on how to bypass the top antivirus products, and it's free.

Now that I'm into your network, I'll gain access to your entire server that will tell me the list of all your users and their passwords for each account. I'll then reuse login information to get me into other accounts, both in the network and social media. Having a company's social media account taken over and sending embarrassing messages damaging the reputation of your company.

In previous intrusion tests, I've pulled out credit card data, client lists, buyer's lists, birth certificates, passports, digital signatures to sign cheques, nude employee or extramarital photos if in the wrong hands can be used for extortion. I can destroy your business.

Step 4 - Maintaining Access: Once I'm in your system, I plan to return undetected as many times as I want. I may even increase the security of your server without you knowing just to prevent other hackers from getting in and undoing my hard work. I could be in there for years, collecting the latest and greatest stuff your business is producing.

Step 5 - Covering My Tracks: Since I'd have complete control of your network, I would then manipulate the network logs to make myself appear invisible. I may even create a diversion to make the IT department think there's a problem somewhere else while I stay covert. When I'm ready, I'll strike.

That's why you got a call at 3 a.m.

IS ETHICAL HACKING EVEN ETHICAL?

Now that you've called in a professional ethical hacker, the question that arises, "is ethical hacking even ethical?" I mean, you are allowing someone to break into your system.

This could involve some sneaky tactics like social engineering, or uncovering their password. It might seem drastic; however, we believe that this is the best method in testing the security of your establishment.

The first thing to know about the hacking community is that it has three subsections: the Black Hats, Grey Hats, and White Hats.

Black Hats: These are the guys you need to watch out for. They hack for the purpose of destruction with little care of the final result. They are usually interested in defacing, stealing, or exposing your information and/or property.

Grey Hats: While they're problematic and have the potential to be dangerous, Grey Hats aren't necessarily trying to wreak havoc. They are more likely hacking to prove they can. However, they still might accidentally damage your content on their way in or out.

White Hats: That's us, the good guys. We're the ones you hire to check and make sure everything is secure in your networks. We have all of the nasty skills of a Black Hat, but we only use these skills with your permission and with your best interests at heart.

To properly test your systems, we need to do everything that a Black Hat would do.

The difference is that you know we're doing it. We are employing a type of esoteric morality that entrusts us to use our skills to achieve the greater good.

To put yourself in the mindset of a Black Hat hacker is the only way to test the security quality adequately.

It is important to outline with your penetration testers the processes that they will go through to test your networks, and have it approved by the most senior executive to ensure the safety of the company.

You also need to understand that they may find access to areas with sensitive information.

However, trusting a penetration tester is like trusting your doctor; we will have you sign thorough contracts trusting us to keep your information confidential.

Many fears for the safety of their country and governments, but how about your businesses? Data breaches are one of the most detrimental problems, a business of any size could experience. Performing a penetration test from Cyology Labs could save companies from serious financial losses, in one of my client's cases, of up to $42.7 billion.

Pre-emptively hiring a penetration testing services firm is an assurance that your company's information and property are completely safe and inaccessible.

You don't want to wait until it's too late.

CHAPTER ELEVEN

ENVIRONMENTAL COMPLEXITIES

Every CSO should have intimate knowledge about their environmental complexities. Environmental complexities mean that companies are still using much older technologies like mainframes and try to make them work with the latest and greatest.

The problem is that they aren't always compatible. The mainframe manufacture is out of business; thus, they can't update their software, leaving it and the company vulnerable.

ENVIRONMENTAL COMPLEXITIES TODAY

If we look at most environmental complexities today, you'll probably have multiple points of access. That includes wired and wireless, Mobile devices, along with analogue/ remote connections such as VPNs or dial-up machines anywhere. We may have an insecure network design which would include a non-infective or non-existent DMZ, or single-layer security design, meaning everything is blocked coming in, but everything is un-blocked outbound. We're not looking at a layered approach. Now we have to worry about new threats and exploits. Exploits are proven ways to get past a vulnerability in computer networks or software.

We need to keep in mind how early someone can start training to attack a network. We can have teenagers attacking anytime. We can have highly disgruntled employees who are motivated by anger and revenge, that given the simple, how-to-use free hacking resources available online, will significantly increase the number of potential threats. Anyone with a broadband connection is a suspect.

New exploits develop as frequently as every four hours. Take Wired Equivalent Privacy cracking, for example, also known as WEP. WEP is found as a Wi-Fi setting in your wireless router. In the beginning, it took several tools to gather the traffic and Key exchange. Now with one tool like Kismet, we can crack WEP in 58 seconds.

It's easy.

There's a minimal focus on security regardless of what people may think. IT Security is allocated the smallest portion of the overall IT budget, and few managers see the need for protection until it's too late.

When we talk about limited expertise, organizations don't want to spend money on hiring expensive security personnel. Most often, security administrations are overworked and undertrained network administrators, given the extra task of security.

There is little doubt: integrating the Internet as part of a company's overall marketing plan is considered a necessary strategy to compete with other businesses. But by making more money comes a new risk: Internet protection against hackers, and that, in a nutshell, means allocating more money to keep these cybercriminals on the outside.

But, security executives are trying to do more with less.

So why are company CSOs reluctant to spend the money?

One way to look at reduced spending on protection is how company executives react after being hacked. As companies experience a breach, as is the case during economic hard times, they may be more likely to spend in the following fiscal year. That's because hard times often means job instability, salary freezes and cuts, layoffs and termination like we discussed earlier.

It's one of those damned if you do, damned if you don't things.

THE THREAT AGENTS?

As the CSO, the biggest threat lies within the company: your employees or users. They are the ones who believe they are underpaid, overworked and possibly unhappy with senior management.

As an example, 21-year old David Ernest Everett Jr., from Blaine, Minnesota, back in 2009, pleaded guilty to computer hacking charges in an American federal court. This young man, a former tech support staffer at the Wand Corporation, was accused of installing malware on 1,000 Wand computer servers and crashing several of them.

Everett admitted that he developed three malicious files, which he then distributed to over 1,000 servers located in various restaurants using Wand systems, intending to crash them. The servers were connected to the cash registers and store financial data, payroll information, inventory, and work schedules. In the end, Wand's security team concluded that Everett exploited a security hole, which he became aware of while working for the company.

To fix the problem, cost Wand Corp. $49,000. The company estimated the losses would have amounted to $4.25 million if all servers were affected.

Investigative Journalist and Author, Richard Tardif wrote in this book's prologue that a Desjardins Group employee in 2018 had "ill-intentions" when he lifted data from about three million people and businesses and reportedly leaked it to others outside the Quebec-based financial institution. All of the Credit Union's 4.2 million members were affected. One employee?

The leaked information includes names, addresses, birth dates, social insurance numbers, email addresses and information about transaction habits.

In another example, ransomware encrypted files of many Fortnite users, despite a 2019 warning of a hack after some players received demands for payment to unlock their computers.

Fortnite is a survival game where 100 players fight against each other in player versus player combat to be the last one standing. Think of *The Hunger Games*, where strategic thinking is a must to survive.

The online video game in 2019 warned its massive user base against downloading a supposed aimbot cheat tool, which claimed to give players an edge over competitors. The supposed cheat tool loaded their computers with ransomware.

Fortnite is an online video game developed by Epic Games and released in 2017. Epic Games advice? Don't download third-party software to cheat.

Other similar incidents involved a former network administrator who hacked the computers of his ex-employer and destroyed data. The objective of the attacker was the hope that he would be hired back to fix them.

Another upset employee turned the email server of the company he used to work for into a spam relay, claiming that he was threatened and forced to resign by another employee of a higher rank. And then, there is, of course, the infamous case of Terry Childs, the upset network administrator, who locked the municipality of San Francisco out of its own multi-million-dollar Fiber-WAN network.

LACK OF EDUCATION

The lack of educated users and administrators can lead to the downloading of infected files off the Internet. Can you say Bit-Torrent? Wi-Fi HotSpot?

In Ethical Hacker Network Magazine, a free online magazine for the security professional, Daniel V. Hoffman, provides a possible scenario.

"You go to a coffee shop for a cup of coffee and to utilize the shop's Wi-Fi HotSpot to surf the web. You connect to the hotspot network and decide to perform some online banking or to purchase something online. By the way, this could happen to you at home, as well. As an end-user, you feel quite secure, as you see the lock in the bottom corner of your Internet browser, symbolizing that the online banking or online credit card transaction is safe from prying eyes. Your data, including username, password, credit card info, etc. will be encrypted with 128-bit encryption. So, it's secure, right?"

What you didn't realize is that the cybercriminal, while you were surfing at Starbucks, has intercepted your online banking login credentials and credit card information. And can now log into your online banking website or purchase items with your credit card.

How is this possible, since SSL was used and is hard to break? The answer is that you made a fatal mistake that subjected you to an SSL Man-in-the-Middle (MITM) attack. The fatal flaw that enabled the stealing of sensitive information is when an end-user is not adequately educated on an easy to do, and well-known SSL exploit – SSL MITM.

Here's how an SSL happens.

The hacker goes to a coffee shop and connects to the same Wi-Fi network as you. He runs a series of utilities to redirect other user's data through his machine.

He runs several other utilities to sniff the data, act as an SSL Certificate Server and to be the Man-the-Middle. Once the user, let us say an employee with a company laptop, clicks on "yes" to the "accept" certificate, the unsuspecting user has just been susceptible to eavesdropping.

CORPORATE ESPIONAGE

Cybercriminals believed to be operating in China compromised at least five multinational oil and energy companies in 2011 in "coordinated covert and targeted" cyberattacks, according to a report by cybersecurity firm McAfee.

A 2011 Heartland Institute online article reports the network intrusions, which have been dubbed "Night Dragon" by McAfee, are believed to have begun in November 2009.

The espionage campaign was designed for compromising competitive proprietary operations and sensitive financial information, targeted email archives, as well as oil and gas field bids and transactions, according to the "Global Energy Cyberattacks: 'Night Dragon'" report released on February 10 in 2010.

McAfee then warned that defence techniques only work if software engineers are motivated or required to use them. There was a brief period of forwarding momentum on security engineering from about 2004 through 2009, but I feared back then we were losing that momentum.

"At the end of the day, there is nothing you can do to deter attacks like these and the best you can hope for is to detect the infiltration activity fast enough to block it and prevent catastrophic data loss," the report stated.

The McAfee report believed many actors participated in the Night Dragon attacks but claims to have identified one individual who provided the crucial infrastructure to the attackers. The individual was based in Heze City, Shandong Province, China, and is believed to be able to help identify those responsible for the attacks.

Here is an excellent place to talk about the 2010 hacking of Canada's financial nerve centre.

Three of the Canadian government's critical departments, including the Finance department, Defence Research and Development, and the Treasury Board, fell victim to what the Canadian government was calling an "unprecedented" and "significant" cyberattack, apparently from "patriot hackers" using computers based in China.

Mainstream media reports say that data contained in the federal Finance Department and Treasury Board computers might have been compromised in February 2010, which would allow financial information on private citizens to fall into the hands of cybercriminals.

Interior sources say that the hackers using servers in China gained control of several Canadian government computers assigned to high-ranking federal officials. Posing as federal executives, (executive spear-phishing), they sent fake emails coaxing employees to reveal passwords. The cybercriminals also sent other seemingly harmless attached memos to federal technical employees.

The moment a recipient opened an attachment, a viral program unleashed itself on the network. The program then hunted for specific kinds of classified government information.

The attacks forced the government departments to disconnect from the grid because the hackers were going after financial records. Canadian officials disabled two departments' Internet connections for a time to halt any loss of data. Are we safe?

The infiltration of three of Canada's critical governmental departments leaves an uneasy feeling in the minds of Canadians, despite then Canada's Prime Minister Stephen Harper's public relations assurance that the government does have a strategy in place to protect computer networks.

In a nationwide broadcast at a press conference in Toronto, the then Prime Minister said, "That he recognized cybersecurity was a growing issue of importance, not just in this country, but across the world."

MISUSE OF "IT" PRIVILEGES

End users or IT Administrators have probably been given too much access and like to poke around the system to see what's there. They can then use this information for personal or financial gain, known as an insider threat.

Every year several data leaks, identity thefts, and cyberattacks are reported in the IT industry, and most often, external cybercriminals are considered responsible for these attacks. But are these company outsiders alone accountable for the increasing cybercrime proportion? Well, statistics prove otherwise.

Stealing of corporate data by employees is a well-known fact.

Dr. Doug Jacobson, director of Iowa State University's Information Assurance Program and founder of Palisade Systems, announced that a new security compliance market, dubbed the content monitoring and filtering market, had been established to thwart internal threats; trusted insiders like employees and consultants who maliciously or inadvertently send sensitive data about their employer and/or customers outside the network without authorization.

"Over the past ten years, thefts of consumers' personal information have been caused by trusted employees and consultants who don't risk the same security barriers as hackers do from outside the company," said Jacobson.

Policies and procedures are only part of the solution to internal threats. While functional, updated policies and procedures help enforce the protection and use of sensitive data, technology will still play a critical role when these policies and procedures fail to stop an employee or consultant that maliciously wants to send sensitive data to an unauthorized source outside the organization.

Content monitoring and filtering technology provide employers with the means to not only control how their employees communicate but also give them eyes into what sensitive data their employees are accessing and trying to send outside the network. What's inside stays inside?

There are other negative consequences an employer may suffer when an employee misuses its equipment and resources for personal gain. The reputation of an employer in the business and the wider community can be severely compromised when even one employee engages in this kind of behaviour, particularly where that employee holds a senior supervisory position.

It can also adversely impact on the work – and work ethic – of the employee in question given the genuine risk that the misuse will occur in whole or in part on the employer's time.

And then there is the threat to a company's information technology systems. Computer operating systems become infected with worms and viruses introduced through inappropriate accessing of pornographic, entertainment and racist websites or through receiving tainted material downloaded from these websites.

NO PHYSICAL SECURITY

The critical areas that all CSOs should be mindful of when designing any security plan are information security, physical security,

security operations, security governance, business continuity, and security management.

There has been a trend in recent years, as the two sides of enterprise security, physical and information, have merged into one singular concept what experts refer to as security convergence. The explanation is that each party has become interdependent on the other. Cybersecurity experts believe enterprises are rethinking the separations between physical security and facility security functions and information security functions.

Many cybercriminals rely on breaches of physical security to aid in their overall intrusion attempts. It's not unknown for these cybercriminals to penetrate the organization undercover as delivery personnel to uncover security lapses to access the network through a variety of social engineering methods.

If someone can get physical access to the system, three of the most common things that can happen is the theft of property or data, theft of identity, and destruction of property or data.

ORGANIZED THREATS

On March 23, 2010, Steven Chabinsky, deputy assistant director of the FBI's cyber division, delivered a speech about cybercrime at the FOSE conference in Washington DC.

Chabinsky says the days of a one-person hacking operation are reorganizing into white-collared criminal cyber corporations, with ties to terrorism. Computer hackers now have specialized roles and skills

By utilizing invitation-only private chat rooms, Chabinsky said that cybercriminals are forming corporation-type organizations that consist of, "associates who respect the skill sets each has to offer and work together to complete their crimes as efficiently as possible."

It's only getting worse.

The organization leaders more often have no actual technical skills. Instead, they act as managers overseeing the general operation. Contractors who rarely know about the process are also a part of the team and fulfil whatever role is necessary at any given time.

Investigators at the National Infrastructure Protection Center, the FBI's cybercrimes arm, warned Internet retailers and online banking firms to be more vigilant in protecting their data.

There are organized hackers, professional cybercriminals and discontented employees out there. The reason for organized crime is maybe to fulfil their political bias, fundamentalism, patriotism, etc.

The Pakistanis are said to be one of the best quality hackers in the world. In the case of professional cybercriminals, money's the motivation.

The Indian scenario of cybercrime is because the Internet in India is proliferating. It has given rise to new opportunities in every field, be it entertainment, business, sports or education. Given the unlimited number of free websites, the Internet is undeniably open to exploitation.

"Any criminal activity that uses a computer either as an instrumentality, target or a means for perpetuating further crimes comes within the ambit of cybercrime," said Supreme Court advocate and cyber law expert Pavan Duggal.

Pavan Duggal is considered one of the pioneers in the field of cyber law and is Asia's leading authority on cyber law.

"Cybercrime is omnipresent, and although cybercrime cells have been set up in major cities, most cases remain unreported due to lack of awareness," he writes.

It's easier than you think. Anyone can do it. Have you ever read this in your email?

Low Risk - High Return - Work Your Own Hours. The Ultimate Get Rich Quick Scheme

It's organized crime, says the FBI. Organized cybercrime has become the most profitable - low risk - high return crime of our age. Hundreds of thousands are quietly using the Internet, hiding behind thousands of infected computers, stealing identities and money from innocent people like you and me, and keeping CEOs and CSOs up at night.

Professional cybercriminals make it their job to take advantage of computer security trends and send out threats like spam, phishing emails, Trojan horses containing keyloggers, hijackers, all targeted to steal your identity and ultimately, your money.

These cybercriminals can work alone or in groups. Either way, their first goal is to infect computers and turn them into zombies or bots. These are computers that the hacker controls without the owner's knowledge.

Anyone can become a part of the organized cybercrime world. The tools of the trade are everywhere. You can find websites that promote the use of these tools.

Organized cybercrime has moved from targeting large businesses to individuals and small businesses. Criminals know that this targeted group has little knowledge of computer security and a small amount of money to invest in their protection.

They view this group as easy prey.

The old saying, "knowledge is power," is most important. Make sure everyone in your home or business understands the threats and is careful not to allow these on a computer. However, even loaded with the best knowledge, there can be accidental leaks from opening a spam email, drive-by-hacking from a website, downloading infected music, and more.

THE COST

Quantifying financial losses from cyberattacks is one of our significant problems. We are still "guesstimating." Sometimes you'll see thousands and hundreds of thousands of dollars lost in an attack, and that's mostly the cost of clean-up and investigation. But the real costs are the opportunity costs: lost business.

If you're conducting e-business and you're counting on $600,000 an hour in revenue, like Amazon, a denial of service attack will disrupt your service. The figure of $600,000 is for every hour of downtime.

If you're Cisco and you're making $7 million a day online, and you're down for a day, you've lost $7 million.

It staggers the imagination, and there's a tendency to disbelieve that four lines of code cost $80 million, or $10 billion in damages. But if you think about it in terms of a 24/7 global corporation, a Fortune 500 corporation, for example, its big bucks.

The Melissa Virus hit a Fortune 500 corporation, and their internal tabulation was that they lost $10 million. How did they lose it? The response is, in most cases, lost productivity and failed network operation time.

Budget wise, they have a dollar sign attached to each minute of network time, and when you disrupt that minute of network time, you cost that much money. And every corporation values its information. This trade secret is worth X amount of money. Once compromised by an attack, then that much money is lost.

CHAPTER TWELVE

ASSESSING YOUR ORGANIZATION

Most small and medium-sized businesses (SMBs) believe they are too small to be targeted. Even those conscious about their security might not have the budget, time, resources and technical-know-how needed to defend against attacks.

This makes it impossible for them to detect security breaches on time, thereby leading to devastating attacks.

IDENTIFY SECURITY AND WEAKNESSES

Cybercrime is predicted to cost companies $6 trillion world-wide by 2021. What's more alarming is that more than 40 percent of those victims are SMBs. Several technology pundits think small businesses are being targeted because they often have more lax security standards than their enterprise counterparts.

Why? Simple, because:

Employees lack proper cybersecurity awareness training, exposing the organization to risk

Their IT is understaffed and overwhelmed, usually wearing many hats, with no security specialists on-site site or the right tools in place.

SMBs are easy targets and usually very good payers, once breached or hit with ransomware, they are the most affected when it comes to extensive automated attacks, large scale phishing campaigns and credential theft.

For these businesses, there is the option of getting a Cyology Labs report card audit. A Cyology Labs' report card audit is uniquely designed to improve your understanding of the level of your organization's security and also identify security deficiencies as well as areas of strengths and weaknesses. Learn more about how this type of audit can help you at https://www.cyologylabs.com/re-portcard.

An audit will go a long way in helping you to:
- Correct security issues before leading to downtime.
- Identify problems that are causing slow performance, frequent virus attacks or communication problems.
- Develop an action plan to correct dangers and reduce the associated risks.

The way to know if you are protecting your business is to know what is happening inside your network. If you aren't currently running regular reports, or your current service provider isn't running a periodic assessment, briefing you on that assessment, and updating your management plan, something crucial might be getting missed.

THE AUDIT

An audit offers a custom security solution built for your business, based on your individual security needs.

My team and I will review your current security policies, work hand-in-hand with you to optimize them (or create a set if they don't already exist), and install cybersecurity software that scans and detects internal as well as external vulnerabilities.

A custom 18-point audit and ongoing maintenance of your network include:

1. Evaluation of your inbound firewall configuration and search for known external vulnerabilities: This helps ensure that the impact of changes made to the external firewall or exposure of outward-facing applications is minimized.
2. Review of your outbound firewall configuration: Blocking unnecessary traffic plays a vital role in eliminating the spread of viruses, worms, and Trojans.

3. Inspection of the effectiveness of your current patch management tool: The purpose of this task is to identify systems in which security patches have not been applied in a timely manner.

4. Examination of your antivirus and anti-spyware deployment: This activity determines where antivirus and anti-spyware is not deployed or is out of date.

5. Conduct administrator review: This review validates the list of users with administrative privileges. Far too many companies give non-IT Administrator users way too much access.

6. Perform physical security walk-through: This in-person walk-through of the office helps identify issues a network assessment tool can't, such as employees leaving their passwords in plain sight.

7. Running an internal vulnerability scan: This uncovers security flaws that could be exploited once an attacker makes it inside your network.

8. Detection of anomalous logins: This task is intended to review security audit logs for suspicious logins or login attempts. This is very handy to see if a cybercriminal is trying to brute force your user's passwords.

9. Assessment of security policies: We'll review your default group policy and applicable local security policies for consistency and alignment with best practices.

10. Review with your IT administrators: This step reviews the user, computers, and layer 2/3 detail with your in-house administrator to identify possible defunct or rogue users and systems.

11. Perform compliance-level auditing: A compliance-level audit can be beneficial in finding security-related, best-practice violations for all companies, even if they are not required to comply with a compliance standard such as HIPAA or PCI.

12. Review of improper network shares: This audit will discover unauthorized users' access to sensitive information.

13. Review of weak passwords: This audit will discover weak/insufficient password requirements and systems with weak local passwords.

14. Review of forgotten and inactive accounts: This audit is great for finding enabled login accounts for ex-employees or vendors. I often gain access to client networks through accounts of employees who left the company years ago.

15. Review of unsupported Operating systems: Are you still using Windows XP or Windows 7 because an important application can't run on new operating systems? This audit will find unsupported operating systems in use on your network.

16. Review of insecure web applications: This audit will find incorrect and inconsistent application security settings, as well as computers with open listening ports.

17. Review of unauthorized devices: This audit will uncover rogue or unauthorized devices and computers lingering on your network. This audit is excellent for finding computers that employees bring in from home.

18. Review of Personal Identifiable Information (PII): This audit will find Credit Card/PII stored on unauthorized systems in your network, such as social insurance numbers and credit card data.

BACK TO THE BASICS

There is a recurring theme whenever there's a data breach. Usually, someone with too much access was attacked, and the person's access was used to move around the company networks. We should remember the basics, come back to them and realize that the more we reduce the attack surface, the less likely it is for your organization to be breached. What are the basics?

- Pay attention to the people you work with and around- Get to know them and maintain contact with your employees, including any contractors your business or building may hire.
- Be mindful of email attachments and web links- Do not click on a link or open an attachment that you were not expecting. If it appears important, call the sender to verify they sent the email and ask them to describe what the attachment or link is.
- Use separate personal and business computers, mobile devices, and accounts -If one of them gets compromised, it will not endanger all of them
- Do not connect personal or untrusted storage devices or hardware into your computer, mobile device, or network- These devices may have malware on them.
- Be mindful of downloading software -Do not download software from an unknown web page. When software or service is free, you are the product.
- Do not give out personal or business information -Social engineering is an attempt to obtain physical or electronic access to your business information by manipulating people.
- Watch for harmful pop-ups- When connected to and using the Internet, do not respond to pop-up windows requesting that you click "OK" for anything. Use a pop-up blocker and only allow pop-ups on the websites you trust.
- Use strong passwords- For systems or applications that have valuable information, use multiple forms of identification, 2FA or MFA.

- Conduct online business more securely- Erase your web browser cache, temporary internet files, cookies, and history regularly. Make sure to erase this data after using any public computer and after any online commerce or banking session. Sometimes we don't want people to delete this in case of a crime. As investigators, this information will help piece together a crime.

Learn more about how this type of audit can help you at https://www.cyologylabs.com/reportcard.

CONCLUSION

The impact of cybercrime on society is creating unprecedented damage to both private and public enterprises, and driving up cybersecurity budgets at small businesses, mid-sized and large corporations.

Cybercrime costs include loss and destruction of data, stolen money, lost productivity, theft of personal and financial data, all disrupting the ordinary course of day to day business.

The costs are astronomical. The Official 2019 Annual Cybercrime Report predicted cybercrime will cost the world $6 trillion annually by 2021, up from $3 trillion in 2015.

"This represents the greatest transfer of economic wealth in history, risks the incentives for innovation and investment, and will be more profitable than the global trade of all major illegal drugs combined," says the report.

By comparison, President Obama's 2017 fiscal year budget proposed a $19 billion allocation toward cybersecurity, which is a spit in the ocean, demonstrating a separation of chasm-like proportions when you consider the amount of $6 trillion.

New technologies are emerging, there's no question, technology benefiting society, every day, ease of use and convenience, but with new technologies, data loss, identity theft, and ransom demands conversely increase. Cybersecurity is an afterthought.

Internet Safety must evolve as new technologies are introduced into society. Throughout this book, we wrote about changes in technology and how it benefited everyday life. We also wrote about the adaptability of cybercriminals in the face of these changes. In my opinion, there are six central themes that will emerge that will be prime for cybercrimes: connected driverless vehicles, Artificial Intelligence in ransomware, mobile malware, the penetration of electronic medical records, the proliferation of cyber espionage, and the illicit creation and spread of fake news across social media.

1 - Connected driverless vehicle: People are embracing the idea of a connected driverless vehicle that would ease their commute but don't realize the cache of data. Connected cars pose serious privacy concerns. Your connected car will know a lot about you, where you go, when you go, how long you are there, the route you took to get there, the route, the temperature of the cabin, what entertainment you engaged, and how long you were chatting on the phone using hands-free Bluetooth.

The experts involved believe that 83 percent of unimpaired vehicle-related fatalities (those not connected to drugs, alcohol, and so on) might be avoided by boosting vehicular intelligence. The belief is sound. Most of the focus has been on preventing individual accidents, but not on preventing cybercrime.

2 - Ransomware: Ransomware: We see evidence of ransomware with artificial intelligence (AI). Cybersecurity analysts have reported that as ransomware attacks increase, a growing number of security experts are using AI to improve the effectiveness of their malware attack defences. The other side of that thought is that criminals will begin using AI to weaponize ransomware and plot more efficient attacks, demanding larger ransoms to decrypt the data.

Ransom payments, typically requested in bitcoins, are also going up. Khari Johnson in a 2020 article on VentureBeat, titled, *How AI is fighting, and could enable, ransomware attacks on cities*, writes,

"Malwarebytes found that the typical ransom attackers demanded from governments and schools in 2019 rocketed up from around $1,000 to over $40,000 by the end of the year. The average ransom by the end of 2019 -over $80,000."

3- Mobile Malware: We'll start seeing more mobile infections as there'll be an increase in fraudulent SMS messages that will come to your phone. These attacks will continue to stem from a username or password, or the SMS code sent to your phone for the Two-step verification. Ultimately, cybercrime watchdogs were already predicting that in 2019, a new era of mobile malware attacks would surface in 2020, mostly mobile banking malware attacks on mobile devices.

4 - Smart Medical Devices: The healthcare industry is going through a significant evolution as patient medical records go online, and medical professionals realize the benefits of advancements in smart medical devices.

As the healthcare industry adapts, there are several concerns around privacy, safety and cybersecurity threats. As more devices connect to hospital and clinical networks, patient medical data and information will be increasingly vulnerable.

Not only are we concerned about patient data going online, but we also have to pray that the hospital's IT staff are doing an outstanding job protecting it. What's even more concerning is the risk of remote hackers compromising a medical device directly connected to a patient.

A rash of ransomware attacks in 2019 targeted hospitals in the US and Australia, froze the computer systems of several medical facilities, to the point where they needed to turn away new patients and even cancel surgery appointments. There are reports in the past of cybercriminals hacking into pacemakers and other various medical electronics. An attacker could theoretically increase or decrease dosages, send electrical signals to a patient, or disable vital sign monitoring.

5 - Cyber espionage: If you've been following the Democratic Party race to the 2020 US election, you may have heard about the US about to wage cyberwar on Russia? It's widely held that Russia was cyber tampering the 2016 election, a concern the US feels will happen again during future US elections. At the end of 2019, over a quarter of companies had experienced a foreign government/nation-state attack. In 2018, 19 percent of organizations believed they were attacked by a nation-state.

That figure increased to 27 percent in 2019. Top future targets will include government organizations, financial institutions, and companies investing in political hotspots around the world. We're at the point now where entire nation-states are using their cyber skills to infiltrate other governments and perform attacks on critical infrastructure.

6 - The Spread of Fake News: Fake news is considered a type of false journalism or propaganda that consists of deliberate disinformation or hoaxes spread through traditional news media. Social media, online sites, is where you'll find implanted fake news. Why is social media the preferred place for fake news?

By clicking on a fake news story, you may be giving hackers a chance to infect your computer or mobile device with malicious software. It's another way of phishing. Once malware is installed, cybercriminals can access passwords and personal information, steal money and even lock down your device.

In March of 2020, during the global pandemic and social distancing, hackers began creating fake news sites with fake news stories with links to malicious websites disguised as COVID-19 maps. Anthony Spadafora in a 2020 article in Tech Radar, *Hackers are spreading malware through coronavirus maps,* says cybercriminals have found yet another way to capitalize on people's fears surrounding the virus, and writes,

"The new malware activates a strain of malicious software known as AZORult. AZORult is an information stealer and was first discovered in 2016. It is used to steal browsing history, cookies, ID/passwords, cryptocurrency and more. It can also download additional malware onto infected machines."

Don't click.

The impact of social media and its vulnerabilities are also seen at home. Cybercriminals are after the data you are storing online at home; they want to get inside your system; then, once in, they will find their way into your company's network; where they can strike, leaving a trail of digital evidence right back to you.

You are also in danger of having online predators after your children, and what, or where, your children search online.

This book has demonstrated that we can protect ourselves by being aware of our online presence, how to manage your social media presence, how to keep your software updated, to strengthen your home network and talk openly to your children, and to take measures to help protect yourself against identity theft.

Whether we are at our business location, carrying company and personal data in our phones, or in a chat room at home, An Insider's Secrets to Internet Safety: Advice from a Professional Hacker, gives you the advantage, control, and peace of mind.

I could have made this book 1000 pages long, but I decided to write it in stages. If you feel that I missed some information, or want to give me feedback, I want to hear from you.

Email me at ask@terrycutler.com, or if you need my help to test the security of your company's IT infrastructure for a fee, or help you remove viruses, you're welcome to call me toll-free at 1-844-CYOLOGY.

Remember to visit Terry.cutler.com for more information such as upcoming courses and products, and I'll see you in the next book.

ABOUT THE AUTHOR

As an award-winning information security strategist for 20 years, Terry has advised Canada's largest companies on how to prevent and remedy internal and external security penetration. For the public, he developed an effective online learning program arranged in modules and updated regularly to keep up with the rapidly changing digital landscape in which "wild-west" Internet bandits seeking new ways to break into our lives are stopped.

Terry Cutler has coined the term Cyologist™ to describe what he does. His mission is to "help individuals and corporations protect themselves from data breaches and other online cyber threats through his videos, media appearances, coaching products, and consulting services.

AWARDS

- IFSEC Global influencers in security and fire 2019
- Named #1 to IFSEC Global's Top 20 Most Influential People in Cybersecurity 2018
- International Cyber Security and Intelligence Academic Award
- International Cyber Security and Intelligence Leadership Award
- Cybersecurity Excellence Award Winner for Educator of the Year 2017
- Best speaker award for content at the 6th Annual Global Mining IT & Telecommunications Summit
- Awarded recognition by the Global Directory of Who's Who 2014
- Technical Book Reviewer - Mastering Kali Linux for Advanced Penetration Testing - ISBN :1782163123
- Robert Scully's World Show : Entrepreneurs/The Dobson Series - Guests: Terry Cutler (#1520)
- Accolades 2012 Award Winner
- Awarded 1 of the top 75 Best hacker blogs on the internet by Feedspot
- August 2009 Pit Crew Award - Penetration Testing Team Hacking, Penetration Testing and Countermeasures.
- Q1/2005 Novell Employee of the Quarter
- Q1/2002 Novell Employee of the Quarter
- 2001 Industry Support Superstar (SSPA - www.supportgate.com)
- Top 10most viewed Article on Canada.com August 15, 2006

QUALIFICATIONS

- Core Impact Certified Professional (CICP) June 2018
- Active Defense, Offensive Countermeasures and Cyber Deception
- Metasploit Pro Certified Specialist, February 15, 2011
- OSCP (Offensive Security Certified Professional) June 2014
- Certified Hootsuite Professional, February 2013
- Certified Information Systems Auditor (CISA), January 29, 2009
- Certified Ethical Hacker v6, November 2007
- Certified Security Analyst/Licensed Penetration Tester (ECSA – LPT)
- May 2007 Computer Hacking and Forensic Investigator (CHFI)
- April 2007, Certified Ethical Hacker 5.0
- February 2007, Certified Linux Professional Suse Linux 10
- October 2005, Certified Ethical Hacker 3.0
- January 2000, Certified Novell Engineer 4.11
- May 1999 Microsoft Certified Professional (Windows NT workstation)
- September 1997   Novell Certified Intranet Ware Administrator 4.11 January 1996 - January 2000   CNE 4 program, Novell NetWare 4.11
- PBSC Internet Training Group, St. Laurent, Quebec

BIBLIOGRAPHY

A Majority of Teens Have Experienced Some Form of ....
https://www.pewresearch.org/internet/2018/09/27/a-majority-of-teens-
have-experienced-some-form-of-cyberbullying/

A Six Step Small Business Cybersecurity Plan | Exchange ....
https://www.ebnemo.com/blog/post/a-six-step-small-business-cybersecu-
rity-plan

Adolescents can stay connected with friends and family ....
https://www.coursehero.com/file/p2chgd1j/Adolescents-can-stay-con-
nected-with-friends-and-family-that-are-further-away/

ANU data breach dating back 19 years detected - Latest ....
https://www.9news.com.au/national/anu-suffers-massive-data-breach-
australian-national-university-news/137debef-392b-44a8-bbb9-
afaa5890d0fe

Australian National University Suffers Data Breach | 2019 ....
https://www.securitymagazine.com/articles/90378-australian-national-
university-suffers-data-breach

Biography of Robert Morris timeline | Time toast timelines.
https://www.timetoast.com/timelines/biography-of-robert-morris

Brunner, John (1995) The Shockwave Rider, Del Rey, New York, New
York.

Canada main target for cybersecurity attacks - IQDATA ....
https://iqdata.ro/2019-canada-is-a-main-target-for-cybersecurity-attacks/

Data breach affects more than 40% of Quebec-based credit union's clients and members. CBC News.

Desjardins announces personal data of 2.9 million members improperly
shared".cbc.ca. 20 June 2019.

Forex and Global Equity Markets - BabyPips.com. https://www.baby-pips.com/learn/forex/forex-global-equity-markets-and-you

Greentel Network. http://greentelnetwork.in/

Grimes, Roger A (2011) Car hacks loom as autos go wireless: Tomorrow's vehicles will communicate wirelessly to reduce accidents, and experts are working to ensure hackers can't abuse the technology. https://www.csoonline.com/article/2622937/car-hacks-loom-as-autos-go-wireless.html?page=2

Grimes, Roger A. (2012) Cybercrime in 2025: New threats mingle with old risks: As our physical and digital worlds become more networked, cyber thieves will use time-tested techniques to pull off scams. https://www.csoonline.com/article/2618635/cyber-crime-in-2025--new-threats-mingle-with-old-risks.html?page=2

Hackers Get Employee Records at Justice and Homeland Security Depts (2016) New York Times, Feb. 8.

Hackers invade Canada - Winnipeg Free Press. https://www.winnipeg-freepress.com/opinion/analysis/hackers-invade-canada-116459663.html

Hackers Penetrate Nasdaq Computers – Infinite Unknown. https://infiniteunknown.net/2011/02/06/hackers-penetrate-nasdaq-computers/ Hafner, Katie & Markoff, John (1991) Cyberpunk: Outlaws and Hackers on the Computer Frontier, Simon Schuster, New York, New York.

Hartley, Rob (2020) Nation State Attacks Are on the Rise. Here's Why You Should Be Worried. https://blog.radware.com/security/2020/02/nation-state-attacks-are-on-the-rise-heres-why-you-should-be-worried/

Herjavec Group (2019) Cyberattacks are the fastest growing crime and predicted to cost the world $6 trillion annually by 2021. 2019 Official Annual Cybercrime Report Announced By Cybersecurity Ventures. https://cybersecurityventures.com/hackerpocalypse-cybercrime-report-2016/

Heroes of Cyberspace: John Brunner - SkyPoint. http://www.sky-point.com/members/gimonca/brunner.html

How a hacker can save you and your business - Groupe Sirco. https://groupesirco.com/en/how-a-hacker-can-save-you-and-your-business/

How to Beat Ransomware - Kindersley Social - Local News .... https://www.kindersleysocial.ca/how-to-beat-ransomware/

How to beat ransomware: prevent, don't react https://blog.malware-bytes.com/101/2016/03/how-to-beat-ransomware-prevent-dont-react/

Info Sheet: Cyberbullying - Public Safety Canada. https://www.pub-licsafety.gc.ca/cnt/rsrcs/pblctns/2015-r038/index-en.aspx

Johnson, Khari (2020) How AI is fighting, and could enable, ransom-ware attacks on cities. VB https://venturebeat.com/2020/02/11/how-ai-is-fighting-and-could-enable-ransomware-attacks-on-cities/

Logic and Time Bombs - zaielacademic.net. http://zaielacademic.net/se-curity/bombs_logic_time.htm

Malware | Online safety, security & fraud | Barclays .... https://digi-tal.wings.uk.barclays/for-everyone/online-safety-security-fraud/malware

Marriott Data Breach Is Traced to Chinese Hackers as U.S. Readies Crackdown on Beijing (2018) New York Times, Dec. 11.

Marriott breach exposes 500 million guests' data - Vox. https://www.vox.com/the-goods/2018/11/30/18119770/marriott-ho-tels-starwood-hack

McCrank, John (2013). Nasdaq forum website hacked, passwords com-promised. Reuters.
Merced, Michael J. de la (2018) Shutdown at Nasdaq Is Traced to Soft-ware". Deal Book.

Montpetit, Jonathan (2019) Personal data of 2.7 million people leaked from Desjardins

Nasdaq and Smug Mug - Smug Mug. https://news.smug-mug.com/nasdaq-and-smugmug-bfbb33b15aa8

Noble, Freya (2019) Australian National University suffers massive data breach dating back 19 years, 9news.com

Prime Day 2019 deals: A complete list of all the ... - BGR. https://bgr.com/2019/07/15/prime-day-deals-2019-complete-list-of-best-sales/

Report: Nasdaq systems were hacked last year | Computerworld. https://www.computerworld.com/article/2513043/report--nasdaq-systems-were-hacked-last-year.html Wall Street Journal

Spadafora, Anthony (2012) Hackers are spreading malware through coronavirus maps Cybercriminals have found yet another way to capitalize on people's fears surrounding the virus. https://www.techradar.com/news/hackers-are-spreading-malware-through-coronavirus-maps

Survival Guide - Infosec Cloud - SLIDELEGEND.COM. https://slidelegend.com/survival-guide-infosec-cloud_5b1a13547f8b9a164f8b4570.html

Terry Cutler - YouTube. https://www.youtube.com/channel/UCEfLy-WUwK3gbUAvg2BPohrg

The Devil You Know: Insider Breaks into the Largest https://ironsphere.com/2019/07/the-devil-you-know-insider-breaks-into-the-largest-federal-credit-union-in-north-america/

The Robert Morris Internet Worm - MIT Computer Science and https://groups.csail.mit.edu/mac/classes/6.805/articles/morris-worm.html

The USB Keys in the Urinal: A Cyber Security Story. https://www.ifsecglobal.com/cyber-security/usb-keys-urinal/

The 2017 Ransomware Survival Guide - Proofpoint, Inc. https://www.proofpoint.com/sites/default/files/ransomware-survival-guide-cm.pdf

U.S. v. Morris. https://h2o.law.harvard.edu/cases/1840

Worm History - Nc State University. https://ethics.csc.ncsu.edu/abuse/wvt/worm/darby/history.html

What Is Adware? - Spamlaws. https://www.spamlaws.com/what-is-adware.html

Why it's time to strengthen your passwords. https://www.mic.com/articles/192829/how-to-strengthen-your-passwords

Windows 8 - Tips and Tricks - Windows 8 and Windows 8.1. https://www.bleepingcomputer.com/forums/t/419139/windows-8-tips-and-tricks/?view=getlastpost

30862484R00098